THE GREAT COOKS' GUIDE TO

Breads

America's leading food authorities share their home-tested
recipes and expertise on cooking equipment and techniques

THE GREAT COOKS' GUIDE TO
Breads

A BEARD GLASER WOLF BOOK

RANDOM HOUSE, NEW YORK

Book Design by Milton Glaser, Inc.

Cover Photograph by Richard Jeffery

Library of Congress Cataloguing in Publication Data
Main entry under title:
The Great cooks' guide to breads
(The Great cooks' library)
1.   Bread   I.   Series
TX769.G73   641.8'15   77-5971
ISBN: 394-73421-1
Manufactured in the United States of America
2 4 6 8 9 7 5 3
First Edition

We have gathered together some of the great cooks in this country to share their recipes—and their expertise—with you. As you read the recipes, you will find that in certain cases techniques will vary. That is as it should be: cooking is a highly individual art, and our experts have arrived at their own personal methods through years of experience in the kitchen.

THE EDITORS

Contents

QUICK BREADS

BREADS: SAVORY, FILLED AND OTHERWISE

Breads

No meal seems quite complete without bread. Take away our breakfast muffin, our crackers at lunch, the crusty loaf on the dinner table, and we don't feel satisfied, no matter how much we eat. There's a good reason for this. Bread is the staple starch of our diet: literally, the staff of life. What pasta is to Italy, what yams are to West Africa, what corn is to South America and rice to China: that's what bread is to the Western world. A famous teacher of Chinese cooking once said that a Chinese meal is properly thought of as a bowl of rice plus some condiments, with every other dish just an accessory to the rice. "But you must know that," she said. "You Westerners have a basic starch, also. Only for some reason you have turned your backs on it."

It's sad but true that in recent years bread has acquired a quite unjustifiably bad reputation. Americans have come to think that it is fattening, unhealthful and full of empty calories, and that the way to be slim is to eat a twelve-ounce steak but to pass up the rye bread. In fact, we now know that the steak contains many times the calories of bread; that it contains little fiber and a large amount of animal fat, and that a proper diet would include a smaller slice of steak and a few pieces of whole grain bread.

Luckily, bread is once again beginning to be recognized for the wholesome food it is. It's full of essential vitamins and minerals. It's low in fat and, when properly made, high in food fiber. When you eat a slice with a glass of milk or a wedge of cheese, the combination provides protein as complete as any you can get. And, in addition, it is filling, delicious and satisfying, providing bulk to the diet at a minimal addition of calories.

It's hard to imagine where bread got its bad name, unless it was as a result of the sins committed by so many American commercial bakeries. We can't blame anyone who stops eating bread when he is confronted with those insipid packaged loaves made of over-refined flour, softened with dough conditioners, stuffed with sugar and preservatives. One solution to this problem is to live in a city that has a large ethnic population supporting bakeries that make traditional loaves. The other solution is to bake your own bread. It's fun, it's cheap, and it makes the house smell heavenly.

So, welcome to the company of breadmakers. Don't be afraid of failure. People have been baking bread for centuries, and they weren't *all* expert bakers. Find a friend who will let you watch her—or him—bake once or twice, and study the description of breadmaking at the end of this chapter. There isn't too much you can do to hurt yeast dough. It's not all that fragile. Even freezing only puts the yeast into hibernation; and unless you kill it with heat, it is going to stay alive. You may have a few failures at first until you become accustomed to working with the living yeast. Our advice is to throw away the failures and try again the next day. A warmer kitchen, a new twist to the kneading, a sudden recognition of the proper feel of the dough, and we promise you that very soon you will have a loaf to be proud of. You will be a breadmaker!

A Short History Lesson: Bread is one of the oldest of cooked foods. If we accept the notion that any combination of flour and water is a bread—pancakes and *pita* and pumpernickel and packaged white bread—then we can trace breadmaking back to the dawn of history. We can see it in that moment when man realized that he didn't have to crunch on raw seeds and grain any longer. Instead, he could grind those grains into a flour, mix the flour with water, and cook the resulting gruel on a hot stone. The results were probably hard and flat; they were undoubtedly longkeeping, since traces of early bread have been found in caves where other remains date back over 10,000 years.

But breadmaking as we know it began, like so much of civilization, in the fertile valleys of the Near East. The Egyptians grew wheat in the Nile Valley, and their paintings are full of depictions of men treading on dough in troughs, kneading dough on a table, and then baking small uniform loaves in conical ovens. (Because, of course, they had to invent the oven as well; without an oven, bread will rise only minimally.) The Egyptians were the first to use leavening to raise their bread, using an ancient sourdough starter in the form of a thick gruel that was kept alive from one baking to the next. And think: if the Egyptians had not had leavened bread, there would have been no need to mention the fact that the Israelites were forced to eat unleavened bread in their haste to flee Egypt during the Exodus.

Unleavened bread still plays an important role in many cuisines. Mexican women wait patiently in line for fresh tortillas at the local tortilla factory (their ancestors, the Aztecs, carried homemade tortillas to the community oven on trays balanced on their heads). In India, women in saris still squat near their bucket-shaped stoves cooking *chapatis* on curved griddles. And who could imagine a smorgasbord without *flatbröd*?

After that, the history of breadmaking is pretty much onward and upward. Better methods of milling and more stable forms of leavening were developed. Different grains were cultivated. Someone thought to add some oil. Another added an egg. One holiday, someone put in fruit and sugar and called the result cake.

Unfortunately, there was another, more insidious development that went along with the diversity of different forms of breads. That was the tendency that appeared, whenever a middle or upper class emerged, to choose refined flours over whole grains. Roman aristocrats were the first to eat bread made from refined flour, and ever since, it has been considered somehow more elegant to eat white bread. Which meant that the best and most healthful parts of the grain were left to the peasantry. The upper classes were able to be so exclusive because the rest of their diet was varied and adequate; still, it is hard to think of the farmers and peasants feeling ashamed of having to eat dark and fragrant loaves of crusty bread.

How Dough Rises: There have been books written about the chemistry of breadmaking, but this isn't going to be one of them. We go by the theory that you're better off standing with your fists knuckle-deep in a springy pad of dough than puzzling over chemical formulas. A few failures—you're sure to have them—and a few triumphs—we promise that they'll come— and you'll know everything that you need to know about breadmaking. On the other hand, you may find it useful to have a simple understanding of the reason why bread dough rises. This is the way it works. Yeast is a living organism and, like all living things, it carries on a process of digestion, during which it takes in starches and sugars that give off gases. You can watch this process whenever you test, or "proof," dried yeast in a cup of warm water with a bit of sugar. The foam that forms on the surface of the water tells you that the yeast is alive, producing gas bubbles as the end-product of its digestive process.

Yeast contains microscopic entities that produce gases when it is placed in the proper environment: it needs water, a warm climate and something to feed on. When you add wheat flour and more water to the yeast, the little organisms start digesting the starch in the flour. But an amazing thing then happens as a bonus. Because wheat flour contains a highly elastic protein called gluten, the gas given off by the yeast begins to push on the gluten fibers and causes them to stretch, making the dough rise.

Punch down the risen dough in its bowl, and you will hear a faint "hiss" which is actually the sound of those gases escaping. Later, when the bread is put into the oven, the gases will expand even more under the influence of the heat, so that the loaf of bread grows larger and larger. Eventually, the yeast will be killed by the heat of the oven, but if you have done your job correctly, this won't happen until it has done its job and produced a beautifully risen loaf of bread.

Now, that is absolutely all that there is to making bread. You can make a terrific loaf out of nothing but a packet of yeast, some white flour, and lukewarm water: only one ingredient more than children use to make flour-and-water paste. Or you can ring in a host of changes: adding rye flour or wheat berries, sweetening with molasses and enriching with milk. The process will be basically the same no matter what ingredients you choose, no matter what variations you try on this trio of flour, leavening and liquid.

Flour: It is the flour that gives bread its character. Have you ever wondered why so many of the breads sold in health-food stores seem so heavy? That's because well-meaning bakers, trying to increase the nutritive qualities of their products, have thrown in every variety of flour, meal and grain that they can reach, with the exception of wheat flour, which is obviously too familiar to be good for you! However, you simply can't make a nicely-risen loaf without wheat flour. It's the only flour containing enough gluten to make a well-risen loaf. To make rye bread, mix rye and wheat flours; make a super-nutritious Cornell loaf by adding soy flour, dry milk and wheat germ to wheat flour; make other loaves by adding oatmeal or potatoes or barley or nut flours. But if you want a bread that rises, then you *must* have a certain percentage of wheat flour, either white or whole-grain.

Once you have learned how to make a basic loaf, you will discover that it is fun to experiment with different kinds of flours. They can't be substituted for one another in equal quantities, since some, such as buckwheat or potato flour, are heavier than others. But if you follow a recipe carefully during your first attempts at breadmaking, you will learn the proper feel of the worked dough and will be able, once you are experienced, to judge the right amounts of different flours by the feel of the dough. A rule of thumb is to use no more than three flours or grains to a recipe; otherwise you won't be able to taste the separate elements. But remember that you must have a good proportion of wheat flour if the bread is to rise.

Yeast: The second partner in the breadmaking process is leavening. Yeast, a tiny one-celled living plant that thrives on moisture and warmth, is the most common leavener. It begins to become active at 50 degrees, matures between 75 degrees and 85 degrees, flourishes between 90 degrees and 110 degrees, and is destroyed at 140 degrees. At first you may feel more confident if you use a thermometer that tells you the precise temperature of the liquid environment of the yeast; soon enough you will learn to *feel* the right temperature. A finger dipped into the water or milk you use should feel slightly hot: not scalding, but warmer than the no-temperature feel of baby-bottle milk.

Yeast can be bought either dried, in packets containing slightly less than a tablespoonful, or in moist compressed cakes. Compressed yeast has a certain prestige since it is used by professional bakers, but in reality it is difficult to obtain, short-lived, and must be refrigerated or frozen. In most instances, it is better to use the dated envelopes of dried yeast that are sold in your supermarket. Brewer's yeast, a by-product of beer-making, has nutritional value but does not work as a leavening.

Other Leavening Agents: Yeast is by no means the only leavening available to the breadmaker. Sourdough starter—a sour, fermenting batter—is added to flour and water and baked, making a moist, tangy bread such as Jewish rye or San Francisco sourdough. Chemical leavenings such as baking powder and baking soda make quick breads, so called because they don't require the lengthy raising process of yeast breads. Serve applesauce pecan bread, or hazelnut pear bread at teatime, or toasted for breakfast. They make a nutritious, not too sweet after-school snack as well. Nor should we forget the flat breads and crackers that are made with no leavening at all, breads such as *matzoh* and *lefse*.

When other ingredients are added to bread recipes, they change the character of the finished loaf but don't greatly affect the rising. The liquid may be anything from the warm water that is used in French bread recipes to syrupy sugars like honey, maple syrup or molasses. Milk is present in many cake-like breads, and German *stollen* can be made with sour cream. Butter and oil coat and shorten the strands of gluten, allowing the gluten mesh to expand smoothly. Salt adds flavor, and sugar, in discreet amounts, helps to nurture the yeast. Breads that contain eggs are a special breed, such as French *brioche* and Jewish *challah,* with tender flaky crusts and golden crumbs. They are less than cake, more than bread, and eating them can be one of life's voluptuous experiences.

A Private Lesson in Breadmaking: This is not a recipe. We won't give you any measurements. What we are going to do is tell you what breadmaking looks like, feels like and smells like. If you don't have a grandmother who can teach you, you should be able to make a decent loaf of bread by studying this description while you follow a recipe.

Set aside a day when you will be home most of the time. It takes several hours to make a batch of bread, but most of the time the dough will be working all by itself; in all, you will spend only half an hour or so with your fingers in the dough. But the first time you make bread you won't know how long each rising takes, and so you ought to start early some morning when you've got a sick child at home or lots of closets to clean or want to watch two football games.

You begin by proofing the yeast. Proofing means testing, and that's all that you're doing. You dissolve the yeast in a quarter cup of tepid water that you subtract from the amount of liquid specified in the recipe. Add a pinch of sweetener to feed the yeast, and take the temperature of the water; it should be between 100 degrees and 115 degrees. Within five minutes you should see that a brownish foam has formed on the surface of the water. That means that the yeast is alive.

Next combine the yeast with all the rest of the ingredients in a bowl. Be sure that they are all at room temperature. Mix everything with a wooden spoon until the dough becomes hard to turn, and then get at it with your hands until you have a sticky dough that can be pulled away from the sides of the bowl.

Now you are ready to knead the dough. That means that you will be working it with your hands in order to distribute the yeast cells evenly and to moisten the gluten. First coat a board or pastry cloth with a thin layer of flour. Then pull the dough out of the bowl and throw it on the board. Dust your hands with flour and work the dough in the following manner: push the heel of your hand down into the dough, stretching it away from you. Fold the far end of the dough back towards you, give it a quarter-turn, and push it away again with the heel of your hand. Knead the dough until it no longer feels sticky. Sprinkle on a bit more flour if you need it. Keep kneading until it is resilient and shiny and, if it is made with white flour, until patting it feels like patting a toddler's smooth skin. This can take anywhere from five to ten minutes. Go at it as hard as you want, by the way. You can't hurt bread dough by forceful kneading.

First Rising: Now wash out the bowl, dry it, and rub some oil over the inner surface. This layer of slippery oil will help the rising dough climb up the sides of the bowl. Place the lump of dough in the bowl and then turn it over so that it has a slick of oil on the top. Now cover it with plastic wrap and stick it away (plastic is much more efficient than the old-fashioned tea-towel). Many books recommend placing the rising dough over a pilot light or in a warm oven; we think that this encourages a too-rapid rising, creating an unpleasantly yeast-flavored bread. Instead, just put the bowl away, out of a draft, until it has doubled in bulk.

It's hard to describe the moment when the dough will have risen enough. You can mark the bowl so that you know the precise height it should attain; like the use of a thermometer, that is a reassuring aid to the beginner. After one and a half to two hours, you should see that the dough has risen considerably under its plastic cover, and that the top looks puffy, rather like a large blister. Very light white-flour doughs actually grow small blisters on their surface. If the dough has over-risen, it will look a little shrivelled on the top, as though it is falling. Stop it when its surface is still smooth. Then you will have the fun of punching it down.

Punching Down: Punching down is one of the joys of breadmaking. Make a fist and whomp right down in the middle of the dough. You will hear the "hiss" of the gases produced by the yeast escaping. Then knead the dough for two or three minutes in the bowl; turn it, and cover it again with the plastic wrap. The second rising, which helps to produce a finer texture, can be as short as a half hour, or it can be eliminated entirely if you are in a hurry.

Punch down the dough once more, and then get ready to form the loaves. You should do this on the same floured board or pastry cloth on which you kneaded it the first time. The easiest way to form loaves in a bread pan is to put in two large spheres of dough; when they grow they will come together and make a comely loaf. You can make a shallow round loaf in a cake pan, or a long loaf on a baking sheet, or a whole collection of elegantly knotted rolls.

Once again, you must let the dough rise, giving it anywhere from 40 minutes to 1¼ hours. Meanwhile, pre-heat the oven. Just before you put the bread in the oven, make a slash or two across the top with a razor to give it a way to rise above its firm skin. Put the bread in the heated oven and spray it immediately with water from a plant sprayer. This shower keeps the outer skin malleable and allows the bread to rise higher. Spray it about five times in the first five minutes and then shut the oven door and let it bake fully.

How will you know when it's done? You can't tell by the size—that develops in the first 20 minutes—or the color—that is dependent on the heat of the oven and the amount of sugar in the mixture. You'll read about thumping the bottom of a loaf of bread to see if it sounds hollow; that's supposed to be a sure sign of done-ness, at least to the ear of an experienced baker. But, for the less experienced, trust a timer to let you know when the bread is done. A little over-baking won't hurt: remember that a thick crust is nature's protection against staleness. Turn the bread out onto a rack and let it cool completely before you wrap it for storage.

Pots and Pans: As you can see, breadmaking is a simple affair that involves a lot of time, a few skills, and little in the way of special equipment. You will want to have a good-sized mixing bowl with rather straight sides for the dough to climb on. As you gain enthusiasm, you may invest in a mixer with a dough hook that will help to take some of the burden of the kneading from you. Then it is best to have a pastry cloth or a good wooden board; various hard scrapers for cleaning the bowls; a thermometer for testing the temperature of the liquids; and a variety of bread pans. By all means, buy one of the new trough-like pans that help you form French bread. And have a clean razor blade handy for slashing the dough and a plant-sprayer for humidifying the oven.

Other kinds of bread require other kinds of equipment. There are waffle irons and griddles, muffin and brioche pans, cutters for forming biscuits and raised doughnuts, rolling pins and mixing spoons.

And that's all. A small collection of equipment and a long afternoon, and before you know it, you'll be turning out beautiful loaves of health-giving bread. Nothing commands so much respect as the ability to bake bread; nothing makes such an enormous improvement in the quality of a meal. Good baking!

Hobart KitchenAid K-5A. If you plan to spend any time making yeast bread, you will either develop hefty kneading muscles, or succumb to the luxury of a dough hook. Dough-hook attachments are available with many mixers, but the KitchenAid K-5A is generally accepted as the best.

Baker's Sheet. A large, professional-quality baking sheet like this one is a must for serious bakers. A heavy-gauge, reinforced-steel sheet will conduct and retain heat well and absolutely will not bend out of shape.

Muffin Tin. The best, most sturdily constructed muffin tins, like this one, consist of individual, seamless cups bonded securely to a heavy-duty frame. To add strength — and safety — to the frame, these edges have been rolled over concealed rods.

Steel Loaf Pan. Heavy-gauge steel coated with tin makes a long-lasting pan that will hold its shape for years of use. The rolled edges and folded ends provide a smooth finish and extra strength.

Brick Oven Bread Pan. A bread pan made of terra-cotta, like this one designed by the Alfred University College of Ceramics, will produce a loaf much like those baked in old-fashioned stone-hearth ovens: high-rising and with a crisp crust.

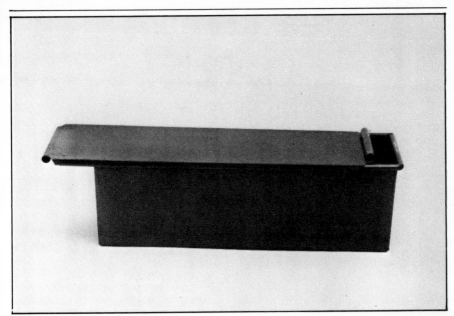

Pullman Loaf Pan. To make a perfectly square slice of bread with a soft crust — just right for sandwiches or canapés — you will need a pan called a Pullman loaf pan. It should be, like this one, of heavy-gauge sheet metal with a dark surface and a silicone glaze (to prevent sticking).

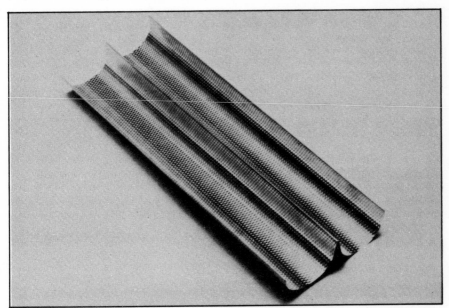

French Bread Pan. A specialty item for Francophiles, this waffled-aluminum pan will make two well-formed loaves of French bread. The pan helps hold the loaves' shape during the final rising and baking.

Yeast Breads and Rolls

AGNES PETERSON'S RYE BREAD

Jane Moulton

3 loaves

2 SMALL RAW POTATOES, PEELED AND SLICED
2 CUPS WATER
2 TABLESPOONS SUGAR
8 TABLESPOONS (½ CUP) SHORTENING OR LARD
½ CUP MOLASSES
1 TABLESPOON SALT
2 TEASPOONS CRUSHED CARDAMOM SEEDS

2 TEASPOONS GRATED ORANGE PEEL
2 CUPS SCALDED MILK
2 PACKAGES ACTIVE DRY YEAST
1 CUP WARM WATER
4 CUPS UNSIFTED BUT STIRRED RYE FLOUR
6 CUPS ALL-PURPOSE FLOUR (APPROXIMATELY)

1. Place the potatoes and water in a small saucepan; cover and cook them until they are completely tender. Pour the contents of the pan into a blender and blend until smooth.

2. In a large mixer bowl, place the potato-water mixture, sugar, shortening, molasses, salt, cardamom seeds, orange peel and milk. Cool the mixture to 105 to 115 F., if necessary. Soften the yeast in water and add it to the mixture.

3. Add all of the rye and 1 cup of the white flour and beat vigorously to a smooth batter. Add enough white flour to make a stiff dough that leaves the sides of the bowl and won't stick to your finger.

4. Turn the dough out onto a lightly-floured board and knead it until it is smooth and elastic (10 to 15 minutes), or use an electric mixer with a dough hook for about 5 minutes.

5. Place the dough in a large, well-greased bowl and turn to grease the top of the dough. Cover and let it rise in a warm place, free from drafts, until it is doubled in bulk, about 1 hour. Punch down the dough in the center and pull the edges to the center. Turn the dough over and let it rise again until doubled, about 30 minutes.

6. Punch down the dough and divide it into three balls. Cover them with a towel and let them rise for 10 minutes. Roll each ball on a floured board into a piece 14 inches by 9 inches. Roll from the long side into a roll, seal the edges by pressing firmly and fold the sealed edges under. Place the loaves in greased 9-by-5-inch loaf pans. Cover and let them rise in a warm place, free from drafts, until doubled.

7. Preheat the oven to 365 F.

8. Bake the loaves for 45 to 50 minutes, or until done. Remove them from the pans and cool them completely on a rack.

   Note: This bread freezes well for up to two months.

BUTTER BRAID BREAD

Nathalie Dupree

2 braided loaves

1 CUP MILK
8 TABLESPOONS (1 STICK) BUTTER
⅓ CUP SUGAR
2 TEASPOONS SALT
2 PACKAGES ACTIVE DRY YEAST
¼ CUP WARM WATER
3 EGGS, BEATEN WITH A FORK
5 TO 7 CUPS SIFTED ALL-PURPOSE
   FLOUR
1 EGG WHITE BEATEN WITH 1
   TABLESPOON WATER
POPPY OR SESAME SEEDS

1. Scald the milk and pour it over the butter, sugar and salt in a large bowl. Let it cool.

2. Sprinkle the yeast into the warm water. Once it has dissolved, stir it into the cooled milk mixture. Don't worry if the butter hasn't melted. Add the beaten eggs and 3 cups of the flour and beat until smooth. Stir in enough additional flour, one cup at a time, to make a stiff dough. Turn out onto a lightly-floured board and knead for about 10 minutes. Put the dough in a greased bowl and turn to grease the top. Cover and let it rise until doubled in bulk.

3. Punch down the dough and turn it out onto the board. Divide it in half and cut each half into three equal pieces. Roll out each piece into strips about 18 inches long. Braid the strips, forming two long loaves. Place them on a buttered cookie sheet. Brush both loaves with melted butter and let them rise until doubled.

4. Preheat the oven to 375 F.

5. Brush the loaves with the egg white-water mixture and sprinkle them with the poppy or sesame seeds. Bake for 30 to 35 minutes, brushing them twice with the egg wash while baking.

CRUSTY DINNER ROLLS

Paul Rubinstein

24 rolls

2 LARGE EGG WHITES (3 IF USING
  SMALL EGGS)
1 PACKAGE ACTIVE DRY YEAST
1 CUP WARM WATER
4 TABLESPOONS SUGAR
1 TEASPOON SALT
3 TABLESPOONS MELTED BUTTER
  PLUS 1 TABLESPOON BUTTER
  FOR GREASING COOKIE SHEET
4 CUPS SIFTED ALL-PURPOSE
  FLOUR
½ CUP FINE GROUND CORNMEAL

1. Beat the egg whites until they form stiff peaks.

2. Dissolve the yeast in ½ cup of the warm water.

3. In the bowl of an electric mixer, place the remaining ½ cup of water, sugar, salt and melted butter, and stir to dissolve the sugar and salt.

4. Add the yeast mixture and half of the flour, and mix at medium speed until it is smooth. Beat in the remaining flour at low speed, then gently fold in the beaten egg whites.

5. If your mixer has a dough hook (for kneading), insert it and knead the dough at medium speed for at least 10 minutes, until smooth and easy to stretch. If you do not have a dough hook, turn the mixture out onto a lightly floured board and knead thoroughly by hand for 15 minutes.

6. Place the dough in a deep bowl, cover it with a damp towel or cloth, put it in a warm, draft-free place and let it rise for at least 2 hours. The dough should nearly double in bulk.

7. Punch the dough down to expel the air, re-cover and let it stand for another hour.

8. Preheat the oven to 425 F.

9. Place a shallow pan of hot water, about 1-inch deep, on the lowest rack in the oven.

10. Remove the dough to a lightly floured board again, punch it down lightly, cut it into 24 roughly equal size pieces (a circular pizza cutter is ideal) and form them into rolls. You may use a braided design, oblong, round or any other shape.

11. Butter one or two cookie sheets (depending on size) and sprinkle them with cornmeal.

12. Place the shaped rolls on the cookie sheet(s), well separated from each other. Cover them with a slightly dampened cloth and let them rise at least 30 minutes.

13. Bake the rolls on the rack above the pan of water for 20 minutes, or until they are golden brown and crusty.

14. The rolls may be served hot from the oven, or after cooling on racks for a few minutes or longer.

TOMATO-RYE-CARAWAY BREAD

Carole Lalli

4 long, thin loaves or 2 regular loaves

1 PACKAGE ACTIVE DRY OR 1
  CAKE COMPRESSED YEAST
¼ CUP WARM WATER
2 CUPS TOMATO JUICE
2 TEASPOONS SALT
2 TABLESPOONS TOMATO PASTE
4 TABLESPOONS (½ STICK) BUTTER
3½ CUPS WHITE FLOUR
  (APPROXIMATELY)
3 CUPS RYE FLOUR
COARSE SALT
2 TABLESPOONS CARAWAY SEEDS

1. Dissolve the yeast in the warm water and set it aside.

2. Heat the tomato juice, salt, tomato paste and 3 tablespoons of the butter, just enough to soften the butter; stir to blend in the tomato paste. Beat the liquid mixture into 2 cups of white flour, then blend in the yeast mixture. Add 1 cup of the rye flour and beat for 3 minutes. Add the rest of the rye flour and enough white flour to make a stiff dough.

3. Turn the dough out onto a floured board and knead by hand, adding white flour as needed to make a smooth, satiny ball of dough. Place the dough in a buttered bowl, turn to butter the top, cover with plastic wrap or a clean dish towel and place it in a warm place to rise until doubled. This will take about 1 to 2 hours.

4. Grease two cookie sheets, four French bread pans or two 5-by-8-inch loaf pans. Turn the dough out onto the floured board and shape it into four long, thin loaves, to be placed on cookie sheets or in French bread pans, or into two regular-sized loaves for the loaf pans. Cover and allow them to double again, about ½ to 1 hour.

5. Preheat the oven to 375 F.

6. Melt the remaining tablespoon of butter and brush the risen loaves. Sprinkle them with coarse salt and caraway seeds and bake them for 30 to 45 minutes, or until the bread sounds hollows when tapped. It should be lightly browned.

Note: If you make the thin loaves, they are perfect for hors d'oeuvres. The regular loaves are good for sandwiches.

CHINESE STEAMED BUNS

Gloria Bley Miller

20 buns

These buns serve as a bland contrast to rich and highly seasoned dishes with gravy. If they are cooked a few at a time, they can be kept warm in a 170 F. oven. They may also be refrigerated, then reheated by brief steaming.

1 PACKAGE ACTIVE DRY YEAST
1¼ CUPS LUKEWARM WATER
1 TABLESPOON SUGAR
½ TEASPOON SALT
4 CUPS FLOUR

1. Sprinkle the yeast over the lukewarm water and stir to dissolve. Then stir in the sugar and salt. Add to the flour and knead until soft, smooth and elastic, about 10 minutes.

2. Transfer the dough to a bowl and cover it with a damp cloth. Let it stand in a warm, draft-free place until the dough is doubled in size, about 1½ hours.

3. Turn the dough onto a floured surface and knead it for 2 or 3 minutes. Cover it and let it double in size once again.

4. Roll the dough into a cylinder about 2 inches in diameter. Then cut it cross-wise into 2-inch sections. Shape each section into a ball, flattening them at the bottom, making them slightly pointed on top. Let them stand 15 minutes.

5. Arrange the buns about 1 inch apart on steaming trays and steam, covered, over boiling water until they are glossy, about 20 minutes. Serve warm.

OATMEAL CURRANT BREAD

Ruth Ellen Church

2 loaves

2 CUPS ROLLED OATS
½ CUP DARK MOLASSES
2 TEASPOONS SALT
2 TABLESPOONS SHORTENING
1 CUP BOILING WATER
1 PACKAGE ACTIVE DRY YEAST
¼ CUP WARM WATER
¾ CUP MILK, SCALDED AND
   COOLED TO LUKEWARM
5 CUPS FLOUR (APPROXIMATELY)
1 CUP CURRANTS, RINSED AND
   WELL DRAINED

1. Measure the oats, molasses, salt and shortening into a bowl. Pour the boiling

water into the bowl and stir to mix. Let the mixture stand for 1 hour.

2. Soften the yeast in the warm water and stir it and the milk into the mixture.

3. Work half the flour into the mixture, beating very well. Knead in the remaining flour gradually, then work in the currants.

4. When the dough is smooth and elastic, shape it into a ball and place it in a greased bowl. Brush the top with oil or melted butter. Cover the dough and let it rise in a warm place until it is doubled in bulk, about 1½ hours.

5. Knead it down and shape the dough into two loaves. Place them in greased bread pans about 8½-by-4½ inches in size. Let the dough rise again until doubled, about 1 hour.

6. Preheat the oven to 375 F.

7. Bake the loaves for approximately 45 minutes.

Variations: Add the grated rind of an orange, if you wish. Whole wheat flour may be substituted for a part of the white flour. Cut-up moist prunes could replace the currants.

CHINESE FANCY FLOWER ROLLS

Gloria Bley Miller

12 steamed rolls

1 PACKAGE ACTIVE DRY YEAST
2 CUPS LUKEWARM WATER
5 CUPS FLOUR
1 TEASPOON SALT
2 TEASPOONS VEGETABLE OIL

1. Dissolve the yeast in the water. Gradually add it to the flour, then knead to a smooth dough.

2. Transfer the dough to a bowl. Cover it with a damp cloth and let it stand in a warm, draft-free place until the dough rises, about 4 hours.

3. Turn the dough onto a floured surface and knead it again briefly. Divide it into two equal parts. Roll out each part into a sheet about ⅛-inch thick and about 14 inches across. Sprinkle each sheet with half the salt and half the oil.

4. Place one sheet atop the other, with an oiled surface against a non-oiled surface. Roll these up—jelly roll fashion—into a cylinder about 2 inches in diameter. Trim the cylinder ends, then cut crosswise into 2½-inch sections.

5. With a chopstick or the blunt edge of a knife held parallel to the cut sides, press down firmly on the center of each so that the ends open slightly. Let the rolls stand for 10 minutes.

6. Arrange the rolls about 1 inch apart on steaming trays over boiling water and steam, covered, for 15 minutes. Serve them warm.

ITALIAN SAGE BREAD (PANE ALLA SALVIA)

Giuliano Bugialli

1 loaf

This variant of the celebrated Tuscan bread is made with the addition of oil and wine to the basic dough and is flavored with pepper and sage. Much of the dried sage in America is of a variety imported from the Balkans and has a different taste than the Italian variety, which is like the fresh sage found in America. Fresh sage may be kept by preserving the leaves under layers of coarse salt.

1 OUNCE COMPRESSED FRESH
   YEAST, OR 1½ PACKAGES
   ACTIVE DRY YEAST
1½ CUPS LUKEWARM WATER
5 CUPS PLUS ½ CUP UNBLEACHED
   ALL-PURPOSE FLOUR
4 TABLESPOONS OLIVE OIL
15 LARGE LEAVES OF SAGE, FRESH
   OR PRESERVED IN SALT
½ CUP DRY WHITE WINE
1 TEASPOON SALT
¼ TEASPOON FRESHLY GROUND
   BLACK PEPPER

1. In a small bowl, dissolve the yeast in 1 cup of the water, stirring with a wooden spoon.

2. Place 1½ cups of the flour in a larger bowl, add the dissolved yeast, and mix with the wooden spoon until all of the flour is incorporated and a small ball of dough is formed. Sprinkle an additional ½ cup of flour over the ball of dough, then cover the bowl with a cotton towel and put it in a warm place, away from drafts. Let it stand until the dough has doubled in size, about 1 hour.

3. Put the olive oil in a small saucepan and warm it over medium heat. When the oil is lukewarm, add the sage leaves, each torn into 2 or 3 pieces. Sauté the sage for 1 minute, then remove the pan from the heat and let the mixture become lukewarm.

4. Arrange the remaining 3 cups of flour in a mound on a pasta board, then make a well in the center. Place the risen ball of dough in the well along with the wine, salt, pepper and the oil-sage mixture. With a wooden spoon, carefully mix together all the ingredients in the well, then add the remaining ½ cup of lukewarm water and start mixing with your hands, absorbing the flour from the inside rim of the well, little by little. Keep mixing until all but 7 or 8 tablespoons of the flour are incorporated, then knead the dough with the palms of your hands, in a folding motion, until it is homogeneous and smooth, about 15 minutes.

5. Give the dough the shape you prefer (a long or a round loaf), then place it on a floured cotton towel. Wrap the dough in the towel and again put it in a warm place, away from drafts, and let it stand until doubled in bulk, about 1 hour.

6. Line the middle shelf of the oven with ovenproof terra-cotta tiles and preheat the oven to 400 F. to heat the tiles which simulate a brick oven.

7. When the dough has doubled in size, remove it from the towel and place it in the oven immediately, directly on the tiles.

8. Bake the bread for about 75 minutes. Do not open the oven door for the first 30 minutes.

9. Remove the bread from the oven and place it on a pasta board standing on its side, not lying flat. The bread must cool for at least 3 hours before it is eaten.

CLASSIC RYE BREAD

Joanne Will

2 or 3 loaves

1 CAKE (.6 OUNCE) COMPRESSED
   YEAST, OR 1 PACKAGE ACTIVE
   DRY YEAST
2½ CUPS LUKEWARM WATER
3½ CUPS UNBLEACHED WHITE
   FLOUR (APPROXIMATELY)
1 TABLESPOON SALT
3 CUPS RYE FLOUR

1. Dissolve the yeast in ½ cup of lukewarm water in a small bowl. Beat in ½ cup of the white flour to make a batter. Let it stand 10 to 15 minutes, or until it is bubbly.

2. Sift the salt with the rye flour and turn it into a large mixing bowl. Add the remaining 2 cups of water and the yeast mixture, mixing with a wooden spoon until it is blended.

3. Add the remaining white flour, about ½ cup at a time, mixing it well with a wooden spoon. When the dough is non-sticky and easy enough to handle, turn it out onto a floured board. Knead in enough remaining flour to make a stiff, yet easy to handle, dough.

4. Put the dough in a buttered bowl, turning to grease the top. Cover it and let it rise in a warm, draft-free place until it has doubled in bulk, about 1¼ hours.

5. Divide the dough into two or three portions. Shape it into loaves and put them into two greased 8½-by-4½-by-2⅝-inch pans or three 7⅜-by-3⅝-by-2¼-inch pans. Cover the loaves and let them rise until doubled, about 1 hour.

6. Pierce the tops of the loaves with a fork or bamboo skewer to release any air. Let them rise 10 to 15 minutes longer.

7. Preheat the oven to 375 F.

8. Bake the loaves about 35 minutes, or until they test done.

ENGLISH MUFFINS

Diana Kennedy (Adapted from and inspired by Mrs. Beeton)

11 muffins

might be O.K.

1 POUND UNBLEACHED, ALL-
PURPOSE FLOUR, PLUS FLOUR
FOR KNEADING
1 TEASPOON ROCK OR SEA-SALT,
FINELY GROUND
1¼ CUPS WARM WATER
1 SMALL, COOKED POTATO (ABOUT
2 OUNCES)
1 CAKE (.6 OUNCE) COMPRESSED
YEAST, OR 1 PACKAGE ACTIVE
DRY YEAST
CORNMEAL

1. Preheat the oven to 300 F.

2. Spread the flour over the bottom of a large baking sheet and dry it off in the oven for about 15 to 20 minutes, taking care that it does not brown.

3. Add the salt to the water and heat to approximately 100 F.

4. Peel the potato and mash it together with the yeast and 1½ tablespoons of the water, using the back of a wooden spoon, until it is smooth. Add this and the remaining salted water to the flour.

5. Using an electric mixer with a dough hook, beat for about 3 minutes (6 minutes by hand), until the dough is stiff but smooth and comes away easily from the sides of the bowl.

6. Scrape the dough out onto a lightly floured surface. Sprinkle it with flour and flatten it into a rough circular shape. Knead the dough for a few minutes until it is resilient to the touch.

7. Sprinkle a large baking sheet with cornmeal.

8. Cut the dough into 11 pieces—each will weigh about 2½ ounces. Roll each piece of dough into a smooth ball. Flatten each ball on the prepared baking sheet, allowing plenty of space between the muffins for expansion.

9. Set the muffins aside in a warm place, free of drafts, to rise for about 45 minutes to 1 hour. They should grow by approximately one-half their size.

10. Preheat a heavy, black-iron or soapstone griddle over medium heat. Just before cooking the muffins turn the heat down to low and lightly grease the surface of the griddle.

11. Very carefully, so as not to knock the proof out of the muffins, transfer, one by one, as many of them as will comfortably fit onto the griddle, allowing plenty of room for expansion. (This should be done with a broad metal spatula and without turning them over. The cornmeal side should be down.)

12. Cook the muffins slowly, as they will readily stick and burn, for 10 minutes on the first side. Turn them over and cook on the other side for 10 minutes longer.

13. Transfer the cooked muffins onto a wire rack in a place free of drafts and let them cool completely before eating them, or storing them in the freezer for future use.

   Note: The muffins should be gently broken open with the upturned tines of an ordinary fork, toasted on both sides and well-buttered before serving hot.

WHEAT GERM YOGURT BREAD

Paula J. Buchholz

2 braided loaves

8½ CUPS ALL-PURPOSE FLOUR
   (APPROXIMATELY)
¾ CUP NON-FAT DRY MILK SOLIDS
1 TABLESPOON SALT
1 PACKAGE ACTIVE DRY YEAST
2¾ CUPS WATER
1 CUP PLAIN YOGURT
¼ CUP HONEY
2 TABLESPOONS BUTTER OR
   MARGARINE
1 CUP TOASTED WHEAT GERM
1 EGG, BEATEN

1. In a large bowl, thoroughly mix together 3½ cups of flour, the dry milk solids, the salt and the undissolved yeast.

2. Combine the water, yogurt, honey and butter in a saucepan. Heat until the liquids are very warm, about 120 F. (The butter doesn't need to melt.)

3. Gradually add the warmed mixture to the dry ingredients. Beat 2 minutes at medium speed in an electric mixer, scraping the bowl occasionally. Stir in the wheat germ and enough additional flour, one cup at a time, to make a stiff dough.

4. Turn it out onto a lightly floured board and knead until it is smooth and elastic, about 10 minutes. Place it in a buttered bowl, turning the dough to butter the top.

5. Cover and let the dough rise in a warm, draft-free place, until it is doubled in bulk, about 1 hour.

6. Punch down the dough. Divide it in half and then divide each half into three equal pieces. Shape each piece into a 16-inch rope. Braid three ropes together; pinch the ends to seal them. Place the braided loaves on a lightly buttered baking sheet. Cover and let them rise in a warm place until they have doubled in bulk, about 1 hour.

7. Preheat the oven to 350 F.

8. Brush the loaves with the beaten egg and sprinkle them with additional wheat germ. Bake the bread for about 35 minutes.

PEASANT BREAD

Nathalie Dupree

2 loaves

2 PACKAGES ACTIVE DRY YEAST
2 CUPS WARM WATER
1¼ TABLESPOONS SALT
1 TABLESPOON SUGAR
5 TO 6 CUPS ALL-PURPOSE FLOUR
CORNMEAL
1 EGG YOLK
POPPY, CARAWAY OR SESAME
  SEEDS

1. Dissolve the yeast in warm water. Add the salt and sugar, stirring thoroughly. Add enough flour, one cup at a time, to make a dough that does not stick to your hands, but that is not tough. Knead just enough to combine the flour and liquid—only 1 or 2 minutes. Shape into a ball and place the dough in a greased bowl, turning to grease the top. Cover with a towel and let it rise in a warm place until doubled in bulk.

2. When the dough has doubled, punch it down and turn it out onto a floured board. Divide it in half and shape it into two long loaves. Arrange them on a baking sheet which is heavily sprinkled with cornmeal. Slash the top of each loaf in two or three places with a sharp knife and brush them with egg yolk before sprinkling them with poppy, caraway or sesame seeds.

3. Place the loaves on the middle shelf in a cold oven. Set the oven to 400 F. and place a pan of boiling water on the bottom of the oven. Bake the loaves for 35 to 40 minutes, until they are crusty and sound hollow when tapped.

ITALIAN WHOLE WHEAT LOAVES

Harvey Steiman

3 loaves

On a recent visit to New York, we were intrigued by the loaves of long whole wheat bread we found in several Italian restaurants. When we got home, we started experimenting with basic loaves and found this to come as close as anything we have tried.

3½ CUPS UNBLEACHED WHITE
  FLOUR (APPROXIMATELY)
2 PACKAGES ACTIVE DRY YEAST
2 CUPS WATER
1 TABLESPOON SUGAR
2 TEASPOONS SALT
2 TABLESPOONS SHORTENING
3 CUPS WHOLE WHEAT FLOUR
CORNMEAL

1. Stir 2 cups of white flour with the yeast in a large bowl.

2. In a saucepan, heat the water, sugar and salt until it is warm to the touch. Add the liquid to the flour and yeast with the shortening and beat with an electric mixer at high speed for 3 minutes. The mixture (called a sponge) should be smooth.

3. Add the whole wheat flour and enough additional white flour to form a rough mass that cleans the sides of the bowl. Turn the dough out onto a floured surface and knead it until smooth, about 12 to 15 minutes.

4. Cover the dough with a bowl and let it rise until doubled in bulk, about 45 to 55 minutes.

5. Punch down the dough and divide it into three parts of equal size. Form each part into a loaf about 13 inches long.

6. Sprinkle a baking pan with cornmeal. Place the loaves in the pan and make several diagonal slices on the top surface with a very sharp knife or razor. Cover them with a towel. Place the pan in a cold oven on the middle rack and place a pan of boiling water on the lower rack. Let the loaves rise for 20 minutes. Remove the towel.

7. Turn the oven to 400 F. and bake the loaves for 45 to 50 minutes, or until they are browned and sound hollow when rapped on the bottom.

NO-KNEAD WHOLE WHEAT LOAVES

Maurice Moore-Betty

3 loaves

3 POUNDS STONE-GROUND WHOLE
  WHEAT FLOUR
2 TEASPOONS SALT
3 TABLESPOONS PLUS 4 CUPS
  WARM WATER (98 TO 110 F.)
3 PACKAGES ACTIVE DRY YEAST
1 TABLESPOON BLACK MOLASSES

1. Mix the flour and salt in a large bowl.

2. Combine 3 tablespoons water and the yeast in a bowl and whisk until the yeast has dissolved. Add the molasses. When the mixture becomes spongy, spoon it into a well in the flour and salt. Gradually add 4 cups of water, mixing with your hand until the dough leaves the sides of the bowl and is rather rubbery. Kneading is not necessary.

3. Divide the dough between three warm, buttered 1-quart loaf pans. Cover with a clean kitchen towel and allow to rise for 30 minutes. The dough should come to within ½ inch of the top of the pans.

4. Preheat the oven to 400 F.

5. Bake for 40 minutes, or until a needle inserted comes out dry. Cool on a rack.

CHEDDAR PULLMAN LOAF

Elizabeth Colchie

1 loaf

Although this bread is good fresh, its very close grain and moist texture make it particularly suitable for thinly-sliced toast for sandwiches or very fine oven-dried Melba toast for hors d'oeuvres.

2 PACKAGES ACTIVE DRY YEAST
1 TEASPOON SUGAR
½ CUP WARM WATER
1¾ CUPS MILK
4 TABLESPOONS (½ STICK) BUTTER
  (PREFERABLY UNSALTED)
4 TEASPOONS SALT
5½ CUPS FLOUR
1¼ CUPS GRATED SHARP
  CHEDDAR (SEE NOTE)

1. In a cup, combine the yeast, sugar and water and stir; let the mixture proof until it is doubled in bulk. Meanwhile heat the milk, butter and salt in a small saucepan until the butter melts.

2. Put 4 cups of flour in the large bowl of an electric mixer and add the milk mixture, beating, then the yeast mixture. If you have a dough hook, add the remaining 1½ cups of flour and beat it in (if not, beat in by hand and by kneading). Knead for 8 to 10 minutes by machine or 10 to 15 minutes by hand.

3. Place the dough in a buttered bowl and turn the dough to coat it all over. Cover the bowl with plastic wrap, place it in a warm, draft-free place and let it rise until tripled in bulk. Punch down the dough, flatten it on a floured surface and gradually knead in the cheese, a little at a time. Replace the dough in the bowl and let it double in volume.

4. Roll out the dough to form a rectangle about 10 inches by 15 inches; roll it tightly, jelly-roll fashion, from one long end to the other. Pinch the seam together and place the roll, seam-side down, in a buttered pullman loaf pan. Let the bread rise to fill the pan four-fifths of the way up the side. Slide on the buttered cover.

5. Bake in a preheated 400 F. oven for 45 minutes. Remove the bread from the pan and place it on the oven rack. Turn the heat to 325 F. and bake for 15 minutes, or until the loaf sounds hollow when tapped. Rub the crust with butter, cover loosely with a tea towel and let it cool completely.

Note: If a food processor is available, grate the cheese in it with 2 tablespoons of flour. If you don't have a processor, grate the cheese when it is cold and firm and toss it with 2 tablespoons of flour to keep it from sticking together in a ball.

PETITE PORTUGUESE BREADS

Elizabeth Colchie

8 small loaves

1¼ CUPS MILK
1 CUP PLUS 1 TEASPOON SUGAR
8 TABLESPOONS (1 STICK)
  SOFTENED BUTTER (PREFERABLY
  UNSALTED)
1 TEASPOON SALT
2 PACKAGES ACTIVE DRY YEAST
3 LARGE EGGS, WELL BEATEN
5 TO 5½ CUPS ALL-PURPOSE
  FLOUR
1 EGG BEATEN WITH 1 TEASPOON
  WATER

1. In a saucepan, combine 1 cup milk, 1 cup sugar, the butter and salt; heat and stir until the butter is nearly melted. Cool to lukewarm.

2. Sprinkle the yeast over the remaining ¼ cup of milk; stir in the teaspoon of sugar. Let stand until it is doubled in volume.

3. Add the beaten eggs to the lukewarm milk-butter mixture; add the yeast and beat in 5 cups of the flour, a cup at a time. Knead the dough on a floured surface, adding up to ½ cup flour, if necessary, to prevent sticking. The dough should be very smooth, requiring about 15 to 20 minutes of kneading. Place it in a buttered bowl, turn it to coat it evenly with butter and cover it with plastic wrap. Let it rise in a draft-free place until more than doubled in bulk, about 1½ hours.

4. Punch down the dough and divide it into eight pieces; shape them into rounds about ¾-inch thick and place them on a large, greased baking sheet. Let them rise in a warm place until the dough doubles in bulk, about 1 hour.

5. Preheat the oven to 350 F.

6. Brush the loaves with the egg and water. Bake them for 30 minutes, or until they are golden brown. Remove them from the sheet and cool them on a rack. The small loaves are rather like very large soft rolls.

Note: This recipe may be easily and deliciously varied by the addition of anise seeds, cinnamon or orange rind to the dough.

CRACKED OAT BREAD WITH CARAWAY

Elizabeth Colchie

2 loaves

1¼ CUPS BOILING WATER
1 CUP STEEL-CUT OATS (AVAILABLE
  IN HEALTH FOOD AND SPECIALTY
  STORES)
1 PACKAGE ACTIVE DRY YEAST
¼ CUP WARM WATER
¼ TEASPOON SUGAR
1¼ CUPS MILK
3 TABLESPOONS BUTTER
2 TABLESPOONS BROWN SUGAR
1 TABLESPOON SALT
2 TEASPOONS CARAWAY SEEDS
5½ CUPS FLOUR (APPROXIMATELY)

1. Stir the boiling water and oats together in a large bowl and let them cool.

2. Stir the yeast, warm water and the sugar together in a cup and let them stand until doubled in volume, about 10 minutes.

3. In a saucepan, combine the milk, butter, brown sugar and salt and heat until the butter melts. Combine the liquids with the oatmeal mixture and cool to lukewarm. Add the yeast and caraway. Beat in 4 cups of flour, a cup at a time.

4. On a floured surface, knead in the remaining flour to make a fairly firm dough. Continue kneading it for about 10 minutes, or until the dough no longer sticks to the kneading surface.

5. Place the dough in a large buttered bowl, turn to coat with the butter, cover with plastic wrap and let it rise until doubled in bulk in a warm, draft-free place.

6. Halve the dough, knead it briefly and form it into two loaves to fit two 4-cup loaf pans (approximately 7½ by 4¼ by 2¼ inches). Cover with plastic wrap and let them rise until doubled, which will reach slightly above the top of the pans.

7. Preheat the oven to 350 F.

8. Bake the loaves for 50 minutes and cool them on a rack.

Sweet Yeast Breads and Holiday Breads

SWEET FINNISH EASTER BREAD

Elizabeth Colchie

1 high, round loaf

6 TABLESPOONS (¾ STICK) BUTTER, CUT UP
⅔ CUP PLUS 1 TEASPOON LIGHT BROWN SUGAR
1 TEASPOON SALT
1 CUP LIGHT CREAM
1 PACKAGE ACTIVE DRY YEAST
¼ CUP WARM WATER
2 TEASPOONS GRATED LEMON RIND

1 TEASPOON GRATED ORANGE RIND
1½ TEASPOONS GROUND CARDAMOM
2 EGG YOLKS
1 CUP RYE FLOUR
3 CUPS ALL-PURPOSE FLOUR
¾ CUP WHITE RAISINS
½ CUP CHOPPED ALMONDS, UNBLANCHED

1. In a saucepan, combine the butter, ⅔ cup of sugar, salt and light cream and heat, stirring, until the butter melts. Cool it to lukewarm.

2. Sprinkle the yeast on the warm water and stir in the remaining teaspoon of sugar. Let it stand until doubled in volume, about 10 minutes.

3. In a large bowl, combine the cream and yeast mixtures, the lemon and orange rinds and the cardamom. Stir in the egg yolks and beat in the rye flour, then the white flour, one cup at a time.

4. Turn the dough out onto a floured surface and knead it until smooth, adding as little extra flour as possible, to keep the dough soft. Place the dough in a buttered bowl, turn to butter the top, and cover it with plastic wrap, letting it rise in a draft-free place until at least doubled in bulk, about 1½ hours.

5. Punch the dough down and knead in the raisins and almonds. Form the dough into a ball and place it in a buttered 1½-quart charlotte mold or deep, round baking dish. Let the bread rise in a warm place until it is well above the top of the mold, about 1½ hours.

6. Preheat the oven to 350 F.

7. Bake the bread for 1 hour, or until the loaf is nicely browned and sounds hollow when tapped. Brush the top with butter and sprinkle it with sugar. Unmold the bread and let it cool on a rack.

GREEK EASTER BREAD

Florence Fabricant

2 braided rounded loaves

2 PACKAGES ACTIVE DRY YEAST
6 TO 7 CUPS SIFTED ALL-PURPOSE
  FLOUR
1 CUP PLUS 1 TEASPOON SUGAR
1 TABLESPOON PLUS ⅛ TEASPOON
  SALT
¼ CUP WARM WATER
5 EGGS
⅔ CUP MILK, SCALDED AND
  COOLED
12 TABLESPOONS (1½ STICKS)
  BUTTER, MELTED AND COOLED
2 TEASPOONS SESAME SEEDS

1. Make a yeast starter sponge by dissolving the yeast, 3 tablespons flour, 1 teaspoon sugar and the ⅛ teaspoon of salt in the warm water. Set aside to rise in a warm place while preparing the other ingredients.

2. In a large bowl, beat 4 of the eggs. (The dough may be mixed in an electric mixer.) Add the remaining sugar, cooled milk and the tablespoon of salt.

3. Add the yeast sponge, once it has doubled, and stir in the melted butter.

4. Start adding the flour, one cup at a time, adding enough to make a fairly stiff dough.

5. Turn the dough out onto a floured board and knead it well, about 10 minutes, until extremely elastic. You should not find it necessary to add much flour as you knead. Place the dough in a large greased bowl, turning it to grease the top, cover and let rise until doubled in bulk. This rising will take about 2 hours, perhaps longer, but it is essential that you do not skimp on the rising time.

6. When the dough has doubled, punch it down in the bowl, turn it over, cover and allow to rise again until almost doubled in bulk. This rising will take less time than the first.

7. Divide the dough in half and cut each half into thirds. Roll each piece of dough into a smooth rope about 24 inches long. Braid three ropes together and form them into a circle, pinching the ends together to join them neatly. Repeat with the remaining dough. Place the twists on a large, buttered baking sheet or in large, buttered round cake tins. Cover and allow to rise until doubled.

8. Preheat the oven to 350 F.

9. Beat the remaining egg and brush the breads with it and sprinkle with sesame seeds. Bake about 40 minutes, until nicely browned. Allow them to cool completely on racks before slicing.

Note: For a traditional Greek Easter touch, gently push 4 hard-cooked eggs, dyed red, into the dough just before baking. The 4 eggs represent the arms of the cross.

CHRISTMAS FRUIT AND NUT BREAD, GREEK STYLE (CHRISTOPSOMO)

Vilma Liacouras Chantiles

1 loaf

Holiday breads are very special in Greece where dried fruits and nuts flavor the dough. In addition, mastic, produced on the island of Chios, lends a distinctive flavor to this loaf.

3 FIGS, STEMS REMOVED
¼ CUP SEMI-SWEET *MAVRODAPHNE* WINE OR ANY SEMI-SWEET RED WINE (OPTIONAL)
1 PACKAGE ACTIVE DRY YEAST
½ CUP PLUS 1 TEASPOON SUGAR
½ CUP WARM WATER
3½ TO 4 CUPS UNBLEACHED FLOUR, MORE IF NECESSARY
1 TEASPOON SALT
1 TEASPOON MASTIC, POUNDED WITH 1 TEASPOON SUGAR, OR THE GRATED RIND OF 1 ORANGE

½ CUP WARM MILK, MORE IF NECESSARY
2 EGGS, LIGHTLY BEATEN
3 TABLESPOONS BUTTER OR MARGARINE, MELTED (PREFERABLY UNSALTED)
½ CUP PLUS 2 TABLESPOONS WALNUTS OR ALMONDS, CHOPPED
½ CUP CURRANTS OR LIGHT RAISINS
SALAD OIL
1 TEASPOON HONEY
1 TABLESPOON ORANGE JUICE

1. Chop the figs and place them in a bowl, covering them with the wine or with water. Cover the bowl and allow them to soak overnight or longer.

2. When ready to mix the bread, dissolve the yeast and 1 teaspoon of sugar in warm water, cover, and allow it to stand until doubled, about 15 minutes.

3. Meanwhile, into a large mixing bowl, sift 3½ cups of the flour with salt, the remaining sugar, and mastic, if you are using it. If you are using grated rind, mix it in with a fork. Make a well in the dry mixture and add the milk, eggs, butter or margarine, the soaked figs and their liquid, the yeast, ½ cup of the nuts, and the currants or raisins. Mix with a mixer or your fingers until smooth, adding more flour to make a soft dough.

4. Transfer the dough to a floured board and knead it for 10 minutes. Place the dough in an oiled bowl, turn it so that the top surface is oiled, cover it and allow it to double, about 2½ hours.

5. Punch down the dough and knead it on a floured board for a few minutes. Form a round loaf and place it in an oiled 9-inch round pan. Cover and allow it to rise in a warm place until doubled; about 1½ hours.

6. Preheat the oven to 375 F.

7. Place the dough in the center of the oven and bake for 15 minutes. Mix the honey, orange juice and the remaining nuts and spread on the dough surface. Reduce the temperature to 325 F. and continue baking for an additional 30 minutes, until the bread has a hollow sound when thumped on the bottom with your knuckles. Cool it on a rack.

Note: Mastic is available at shops specializing in herbs and spices, and also at Greek and Middle Eastern groceries.

KULICH

Carol Cutler

2 high, round loaves

Kulich is a Russian brioche-type bread enjoyed the year round, but obligatory for the Easter table. It is made to accompany another traditional Easter dessert, *paskha,* the rich, molded sweet made of a cheese similar to cottage cheese. They make a pretty pair: the pyramidal *paskha* placed beside the puffy, mushroom-shaped *kulich.* Both are sliced horizontally from the top down, disappearing together to the great pleasure of family and friends.

2 PACKAGES ACTIVE DRY YEAST
½ CUP WARM WATER
1 TEASPOON PLUS ½ CUP SUGAR
8 TABLESPOONS (1 STICK) BUTTER
1¼ CUPS MILK
4 CUPS FLOUR
1 TABLESPOON SALT
2 EGGS, BEATEN
1 EGG YOLK, BEATEN
CONFECTIONERS' SUGAR

1. In a warm bowl, combine the yeast, warm water and 1 teaspoon of sugar. Stir until the yeast is dissolved, and set it aside.

2. In a deep bowl, put ½ cup of sugar and the butter. Heat the milk until it is almost boiling and pour it over the sugar and butter. Stir to dissolve the sugar and set it aside to cool to lukewarm, then add the yeast mixture to the milk.

3. Sift the flour and salt together into a large bowl and add the milk mixture slowly while beating. Add the 2 eggs. When all the liquid is well mixed in, knead the dough until it is smooth and elastic. Place the dough in a clean bowl, cover and put it in a warm place to rise until it is doubled in bulk, about 2 hours.

4. Turn the dough out onto a floured work surface. Cut off a small piece for the decoration and work the rest into a large ball. Divide the dough in half and place it in two large, well-buttered cylindrical baking tins (two 2-pound coffee tins will do).

5. Roll out the reserved piece of dough and cut it into six long ½-inch-wide strips. Make two braids of three strips each and place each in a circle on top of the dough. Allow the dough to rise again for ½ hour.

6. Preheat the oven to 350 F. Brush the tops of the loaves with beaten egg yolk and bake for about 40 minutes, or until the tops have browned nicely and are puffed.

7. Let the bread cool slightly, then remove them from the tins. When the *kulichs* are completely cool, spread the tops with a white icing made of a mixture of confectioners' sugar and water.

8. To serve, cut off the top puff horizontally and set it aside. Slice the rest horizontally with a bread knife, and return the top to keep the *kulich* moist and fresh.

GREEK NEW YEAR'S DAY SWEET BREAD
(VASILOPITA)

Vilma Liacouras Chantiles

1 round loaf

Typical of special holiday breads, *Vasilopita* (St. Basil's *pita*) is prepared where-ever Hellenes live. The *Vasilopita* is characterized by the "lucky coin" hidden inside. The ritual slicing is done by the head of the family, and the family member who finds the coin receives a special blessing. Originating in Asia Minor, this version is like a cake—soft chestnut-layered crust, and subtly-flavored, yellow grain.

1 PACKAGE ACTIVE DRY YEAST
1 CUP PLUS ½ TEASPOON SUGAR
1¼ CUPS WARM MILK
5¼ TO 5¾ CUPS UNBLEACHED
  FLOUR
1 TEASPOON SALT
3 MEDIUM-SIZED EGGS, LIGHTLY
  BEATEN
1 CUP (2 STICKS) BUTTER OR
  MARGARINE, MELTED
  (PREFERABLY UNSALTED)

1 TEASPOON *MAHLEPI* SEEDS,
  BOILED FOR 3 MINUTES IN ⅓
  CUP OF WATER (SEE NOTE
  BELOW)
SALAD OIL
"LUCKY COIN" (DIME, QUARTER,
  OR GOLD PIECE) WASHED AND
  WRAPPED IN WAXED PAPER
  (OPTIONAL)
SESAME SEEDS

1. In a small bowl, dissolve the yeast and ½ teaspoon of the sugar in ½ cup milk. Cover and allow it to double, about 15 minutes.

2. Meanwhile, combine the 5¼ cups of flour, the remaining sugar, and salt in a large mixing bowl. Make a well in the center and pour in all except 2 table-spoons of the beaten eggs (reserve it for the glaze), the butter, the strained, still-warm *mahlepi* water, the remaining milk, and the yeast. Mix to form a soft dough, adding more flour if necessary.

3. Transfer to a floured board. Knead until smooth and satiny. Place the dough in an oiled bowl and turn it to oil the top. Cover and let it rise until it is doubled in bulk, about 2½ hours.

4. Punch down the dough and knead it on the floured board for a minute or two. Shape it into a round loaf. If you are using the "lucky coin," slip it into the bottom of the loaf and pinch the opening closed. Oil a 10-inch round pan and place the dough in the pan. Cover and allow it to double, about 1½ hours.

5. Preheat the oven to 400 F.

6. To decorate the loaf, use kitchen shears to clip garland designs in the sur-face of the dough that curve toward the center top. Brush the bread with the reserved egg and dust it liberally with sesame seeds. Bake for 10 minutes, then reduce the heat to 350 F. and continue baking for 30 minutes. Reduce the heat to 325 F. and bake for a final 10 minutes. If the crust is browning too quickly after 30 minutes, reduce the heat to 325 F. Cool on a rack.

Note: Mahlepi is available in Greek and Middle Eastern shops. The seeds are discarded after boiling. *Mahlepi* imparts a delicate flavor.

SAFFRON TEA BREAD

Maurice Moore-Betty

2 loaves

3 POUNDS FLOUR
1 TEASPOON NUTMEG
2 TEASPOONS SALT
1¼ TEASPOONS SAFFRON THREADS
2 CUPS WARM WATER
1 OUNCE COMPRESSED YEAST,
  OR 1½ PACKAGES ACTIVE DRY
  YEAST
1 POUND (4 STICKS) BUTTER
½ CUP BROWN SUGAR
3 EGGS
1 POUND CURRANTS
½ CUP CHOPPED CANDIED LEMON
  PEEL

1. Sift the flour, nutmeg and salt together in a large bowl.

2. Soak the saffron in the warm water for 20 minutes, then strain it, reserving the liquid. Remove ½ cup of the liquid and crumble or sprinkle the yeast over it to soften it.

3. Reheat the remaining 1½ cups saffron water and melt the butter and dissolve the sugar in it.

4. Beat the eggs until they are frothy and add them to the flour along with the softened yeast and the saffron water-butter mixture. Stir together to form a dough. Fold in the currants and the candied lemon peel and knead lightly. Gather the dough into a mound and place it in a covered bowl to rise until it is doubled in size.

5. Preheat the oven to 400 F.

6. Punch down the dough and shape it into two loaves. Bake in 1½-quart, greased loaf pans for 1½ hours. Test for doneness with a toothpick, which should come out dry. Cool the loaves on a wire rack.

SOURDOUGH COFFEE CAKE

Emanuel and Madeline Greenberg

1 loaf

Sourdough Starter:
1½ CUPS LUKEWARM WATER
1 PACKAGE ACTIVE DRY YEAST
1½ CUPS FLOUR
1 TABLESPOON SUGAR

1. Pour ½ cup of the water into a glass or crockery container and sprinkle it with the yeast. Let it stand for 5 minutes.

2. Add the remaining water, the flour and sugar and mix it well.

3. Cover the container lightly and put it in a warm place, stirring it occasionally. The mixture will become bubbly and have a pleasantly sour aroma. This takes 2 to 4 days.

4. The starter is now ready to be used. After measuring out the amount needed, stir an equal amount of flour and water into the remaining starter. Refrigerate it, lightly covered, for further use.

Coffee Cake:
11 TABLESPOONS (1 STICK PLUS 3
   TABLESPOONS) BUTTER
1½ CUPS SUGAR
3 EGGS
1 CUP SOURDOUGH STARTER
2½ CUPS FLOUR
1½ TEASPOONS BAKING SODA
½ TEASPOON BAKING POWDER
½ TEASPOON SALT
¾ CUP COFFEE

1. Preheat the oven to 350 F.

2. Cream the butter and sugar together until fluffy. Beat in the eggs, one at a time. Stir in the sourdough starter.

3. Lightly toss the dry ingredients together. Add to the butter mixture alternately with the coffee, beating well after each addition. Spoon the batter into a greased and floured 10-inch tube or bundt pan.

4. Bake for 55 to 60 minutes, or until a toothpick inserted in the cake comes out clean. Cool in the pan about 10 minutes, then turn it out on a rack to cool completely.

Note: This is delicious toasted.

ITALIAN PEPPERED FRUIT BREAD
(PANPEPATO)

Giuliano Bugialli

1 loaf

Panpepato has been eaten in central Italy since at least 1300, the date of the earliest manuscript recipe for it. It is probably the original ancestor of English and American fruitcake and plum-pudding. Originally the dough was allowed to rise; some later versions omit this. The chocolate was added about 200 years ago. Despite modern prejudices against the medieval mixture of "hot" and "sweet," the bread has hung on as a traditional snack in central Italy to the present day.

1 OUNCE COMPRESSED FRESH YEAST, OR 1½ PACKAGES ACTIVE DRY YEAST
4 CUPS LUKEWARM WATER
4 CUPS PLUS ½ CUP OF UN- BLEACHED ALL-PURPOSE FLOUR
½ CUP RAISINS
½ CUP SHELLED BLANCHED WALNUTS
½ CUP SHELLED BLANCHED ALMONDS
½ CUP CHOCOLATE CHIPS
½ CUP MIXED GLAZED FRUIT
½ CUP HONEY
½ CUP PITTED DATES
1⅓ TABLESPOONS OLIVE OIL
½ TEASPOON SALT
1 TEASPOON FRESHLY GROUND BLACK PEPPER
SCANT ½ TEASPOON FRESHLY GROUND NUTMEG

1. Dissolve the yeast in 1 cup of the water in a small bowl, stirring with a wooden spoon.

2. Place 1½ cups of flour in a larger bowl, add the dissolved yeast, and mix with a wooden spoon until all the flour is incorporated and a small ball of dough is formed. Sprinkle an additional ½ cup of flour over the ball of dough, then cover the bowl with a cotton towel and put it in a warm place, away from drafts. Let it stand until the dough has doubled in size, about 1 hour.

3. While the dough is rising, soak the raisins in a small bowl with 2 cups of lukewarm water for 1 hour.

4. Chop the walnuts and almonds into small pieces and place them in a large bowl. Add the chocolate chips, glazed fruit and honey to the bowl. Cut each date into 4 pieces and add them to the bowl.

5. Sprinkle 1 tablespoon of the olive oil and the salt, pepper and nutmeg over the contents of the bowl. Mix all the ingredients together with a wooden spoon.

6. When the dough has doubled in size, add it to the nut and fruit mixture, along with the drained raisins, mixing carefully with a wooden spoon. Then add 1 cup of lukewarm water and the 2 cups of flour, little by little, while mixing very gently for about 10 minutes.

7. With the remaining oil, oil and flour an 8-inch diameter spring-form pan and place the dough in it. Cover the pan with a cotton towel and put it in a warm place away from drafts, to double in size, about 1 hour.

8. Preheat the oven to 400 F.

9. When the dough has doubled in size, immediately place the pan in the pre-heated oven and bake for about 65 minutes.

10. Take the bread from the oven, open the spring-form immediately and re-move the bread to a wooden surface.

   Note: This bread is generally not eaten until at least 1 day after it is baked.

STREUSEL BUNDT KUCHEN

Emanuel and Madeline Greenberg

1 loaf

2 ENVELOPES ACTIVE DRY YEAST
¼ CUP WARM WATER
¾ CUP WARM MILK
3¼ CUPS SIFTED FLOUR
8 TABLESPOONS (1 STICK) BUTTER
½ CUP SUGAR
4 EGGS
1 TEASPOON VANILLA
¼ TEASPOON NUTMEG
1 TEASPOON SALT

Streusel:
1 CUP BROWN SUGAR, PACKED
3 TABLESPOONS FLOUR
½ TEASPOON CINNAMON
3 TABLESPOONS BUTTER
½ CUP CHOPPED NUTS

1. Dissolve the yeast in the water. Add the milk and 1 cup of the flour. Beat well. Cover with a towel and let rise in a warm place until doubled in bulk.

2. Cream the butter with the sugar. Beat in the eggs, one at a time. Add the vanilla. Stir the butter mixture into the raised dough. Sift the remaining flour with the nutmeg and the salt. Add to the dough, mixing very well.

3. Combine the brown sugar, flour and cinnamon for the *streusel*. Cut in the but-ter with a pastry blender or two knives. Add the nuts.

4. Put about ⅓ of the dough in a well-greased 10-inch bundt pan. Sprinkle with half of the *streusel* mixture. Add another third of the dough and sprinkle with the rest of the *streusel*. Add the remaining dough to the pan. Cover and let rise until it is doubled in bulk.

5. Preheat the oven to 350 F.

6. Bake for 45 to 50 minutes. Cool in the pan about 10 minutes, then turn out on a rack to cool completely.

Quick Breads

HAZELNUT AND PEAR BREAKFAST LOAF

Elizabeth Colchie

1 loaf

½ CUP SHELLED HAZELNUTS
(FILBERTS)
8 TABLESPOONS (1 STICK)
SOFTENED BUTTER
(PREFERABLY UNSALTED)
½ CUP SUGAR
½ CUP LIGHT BROWN SUGAR
2 LARGE EGGS
1 LARGE BOSC PEAR
2 TABLESPOONS LEMON JUICE

¾ TEASPOON GRATED LEMON
RIND
1¾ CUPS FLOUR
1 TEASPOON DOUBLE-ACTING
BAKING POWDER
½ TEASPOON BAKING SODA
1 TABLESPOON GROUND
CORIANDER
½ TEASPOON SALT

1. Spread the nuts on a baking pan and bake at 350 F. for 20 minutes. Cool a few minutes, then rub them together in handfuls in a towel to remove most of the husks. Cool completely and chop them fine.

2. In the bowl of an electric mixer, cream the butter until it is light. Slowly add the sugars, beating constantly, until the mixture is light and fluffy. Beat in the eggs, one at a time.

3. Grate enough pear to measure 1¼ cups, toss it with the lemon juice and add it to the bowl of the mixer with the lemon rind.

4. Preheat the oven to 350 F.

5. Sift together the flour, baking powder, baking soda, coriander and salt. With the machine set at the lowest speed, gradually beat the sifted ingredients into the batter. Fold in the nuts. Spread the batter in a buttered and lightly floured 9-by-5-by-3-inch loaf pan.

6. Bake the loaf in the center of the oven for 1 hour. Cool it for 10 minutes. Unmold the loaf on a rack and cool it completely. Wrap it tightly in plastic wrap and keep it overnight or longer before serving.

GINGERBREAD

Joanne Will

9 servings

This is more like bread than cake. Serve it with butter or whipped cream cheese.

1½ CUPS FLOUR
1 TEASPOON CINNAMON
1 TEASPOON BAKING SODA
½ TEASPOON GINGER
⅛ TEASPOON SALT
2 EGGS
¾ CUP SUGAR
2 TABLESPOONS MOLASSES
1 CUP SOUR CREAM

1. Preheat the oven to 350 F.

2. Sift together the flour, cinnamon, baking soda, ginger, and salt.

3. Beat the eggs, sugar, and molasses in the large bowl of an electric mixer. Add the sifted dry ingredients, alternating with the sour cream, beginning and ending with flour. Beat the mixture just until blended and smooth.

4. Turn the batter into a greased 8-by-8-by-2-inch pan. Bake for 30 minutes. Serve warm.

PARMESAN POPOVERS

Michael Batterberry

12 to 14 popovers

1 CUP FLOUR
¾ CUP MILK
2 EGGS
1 TEASPOON SALT
3 TABLESPOONS GRATED
  PARMESAN CHEESE
SALAD OIL

1. Preheat the oven to 425 F.

2. With a whisk, stir together the first four ingredients until quite smooth; don't worry about a few small stubborn lumps.

3. Add the cheese, stirring just enough to distribute it evenly.

4. Grease the depressions in a popover pan with salad oil. Fill them three-quarters full with batter and bake for 20 to 25 minutes. The popovers will have risen and turned a rich dark gold.

BEER BREAD

Jane Moulton

1 loaf

3½ CUPS SELF-RISING FLOUR
¼ CUP SUGAR
1 CAN (12 OUNCES) BEER, AT
  ROOM TEMPERATURE
1 EGG

1. Preheat the oven to 375 F.

2. In a mixing bowl, place the flour. (Measure it by spooning it into a cup and leveling the surface with a knife. Don't shake it down.) Add the sugar and stir well with a spoon.

3. Add the beer all at once and, before stirring, break the egg into it. Mix the egg into the beer on the surface of the flour and then stir into the flour with a spoon. Stir just long enough to mix well.

4. Put the batter into a greased 9-by-5-inch loaf pan and bake for 65 to 70 minutes, or until done. Remove the bread from the pan and cool it on a rack.

Note: This makes a bread with a crusty and rough surface and compact interior. It's good warm from the oven and delicious toasted.

RICH SHORT BISCUITS

Helen McCully

18 biscuits

These are delicious with a cup of hot tea and some homemade jam.

2 CUPS ALL-PURPOSE FLOUR
2 TEASPOONS BAKING POWDER
1 TEASPOON SALT
4 TABLESPOONS (½ STICK)
  BUTTER, CUT UP
⅔ CUP MILK

1. Preheat the oven to 450 F.

2. Sift the flour, baking powder and salt together into a large bowl. Add the butter and cut it in with a pastry blender until the mixture is mealy. Stir in the milk with a fork and mix just long enough to combine the ingredients.

3. Turn the dough out onto a lightly-floured pastry cloth. Knead it for a few seconds. Pat the dough to a thickness of about ½ inch and cut it into circles with a 2-inch cookie cutter.

4. Place the dough circles on an ungreased baking sheet, leaving space between them. Bake for 12 to 15 minutes.

Three notes: 1) Contrary to popular belief, the pan need not be heated before spooning in the batter; 2) Because of the cheese and double-the-usual amount of egg, these popovers do not rise as high as the plain ones. Possibly "puffovers" would be a more accurate name for them. They demand to be served with the freshest, finest sweet butter available; and 3) They can also be made in little greased custard cups set on a cookie sheet.

PUMPKIN WHOLE WHEAT QUICK BREAD

Elizabeth Colchie

1 loaf

1 CUP PUMPKIN PURÉE
1 CUP LIGHT BROWN SUGAR
6 TABLESPOONS (¾ STICK) BUTTER, MELTED AND SLIGHTLY BROWNED
1 LARGE EGG AND 1 EGG YOLK, BEATEN TOGETHER
⅓ CUP APPLE CIDER
1¾ CUPS FLOUR

1 TABLESPOON DOUBLE-ACTING BAKING POWDER
1½ TEASPOONS CINNAMON
½ TEASPOON SALT
½ CUP WHOLE WHEAT FLOUR
½ CUP CHOPPED PECANS, LIGHTLY TOASTED
½ CUP YELLOW RAISINS

1. Preheat the oven to 325 F.

2. In a large bowl, stir together the purée, brown sugar, butter, eggs and cider until the sugar dissolves. Into a bowl, sift together the flour, baking powder, cinnamon and salt; stir in the whole wheat flour, pecans and raisins. Gradually add the dry ingredients to the pumpkin mixture, stirring just to blend evenly—do not beat.

3. Turn the batter into a greased and floured loaf pan, approximately 9-by-5-by-3 inches; smooth the top with a wet spatula. Bake for 1 hour, or until a skewer or cake tester inserted in the center comes out clean. Cool 5 minutes and unmold on a rack to cool completely. Wrap the loaf in plastic wrap and keep at least one day before serving.

BLUEBERRY MUFFINS

Helen McCully

1½ CUPS FLOUR
1 CUP FRESH OR DRY FLASH-
   FROZEN BLUEBERRIES
1 EGG
½ CUP MILK
2 TABLESPOONS MELTED BUTTER
2 TEASPOONS BAKING POWDER
½ TEASPOON SALT
½ CUP SUGAR

1. Preheat the oven to 400 F.

2. Butter a 12-cup muffin tin well. Set it aside. Mix ¼ cup of the flour with the blueberries and set them aside.

3. Beat the egg lightly in a mixing bowl. Stir in the milk and melted butter.

4. Sift the remaining flour, baking powder, salt and sugar over the egg mixture. Stir just long enough to moisten the flour. (The batter will look lumpy but that's par for the muffin course. Over-mixing muffins will ruin them.) Finally, fold in the blueberries.

5. Fill the prepared muffin tins two-thirds full. Bake for 20 to 25 minutes. Serve hot with lots of butter.

JALAPEÑO CORN BREAD

Nan Mabon

8 servings

This is a nice accompaniment to chili con carne.

1 CUP FLOUR
4 TEASPOONS BAKING POWDER
2 TABLESPOONS SUGAR
1 TEASPOON SALT
1½ CUPS YELLOW CORNMEAL
2 EGGS
1 CUP BUTTERMILK
1 MEDIUM-SIZED ONION, GRATED

3 TABLESPOONS MELTED LARD OR
   BUTTER
2 CUPS GRATED SHARP CHEDDAR
   CHEESE
1 7-OUNCE CAN JALAPEÑO
   PEPPERS, DRAINED AND
   CHOPPED

1. Preheat the oven to 400 F.

2. Sift the flour, baking powder, sugar, and salt together into a mixing bowl and add the cornmeal. Beat the eggs and stir them into the dry ingredients along with the buttermilk, grated onion and 1 tablespoon of the melted lard or butter.

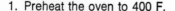

3. Heat the remaining lard or butter in a 9-inch cast-iron skillet and pour in half the corn bread batter, smoothing it over the bottom of the pan with a knife.

4. Sprinkle 1 cup of the cheese and the jalapeño peppers on the batter and then add the remaining batter. Sprinkle with the remaining cheese and place the skillet in the oven for 30 minutes.

5. Run a knife around the edge of the pan to loosen the bread, then flip it over onto a plate. Place the serving plate over the bread and flip it again, so that the cheese side of the corn bread is up. Serve it hot with plenty of butter.

CRANBERRY-ORANGE TEA BREAD

Elizabeth Colchie

1 loaf

½ CUP WALNUTS, COARSELY CHOPPED
2¼ CUPS ALL-PURPOSE FLOUR
1 TEASPOON DOUBLE-ACTING BAKING POWDER
¾ TEASPOON BAKING SODA
¼ TEASPOON SALT
2 CUPS CRANBERRIES, CHOPPED
4 TEASPOONS GRATED ORANGE PEEL

8 TABLESPOONS (1 STICK) SOFTENED BUTTER (PREFERABLY UNSALTED)
¾ CUP SUGAR
¼ CUP HONEY
2 LARGE EGGS
⅓ CUP FRESH ORANGE JUICE

1. Toast the chopped walnuts in a baking pan in a 300 F. oven for 15 minutes. Allow them to cool.

2. Sift the flour, baking powder, baking soda and salt together into a bowl. In a small bowl, combine the cranberries, the orange peel and the nuts.

3. In the bowl of an electric mixer, cream the butter until it is light; add the sugar and honey gradually, beating the mixture until it is very light. Add the eggs, one at a time. Add the flour mixture (reserving ¼ cup) at lowest speed, alternating it with the orange juice.

4. Toss the berry mixture with the reserved flour, and fold it into the batter.

5. Preheat the oven to 350 F.

6. Turn the batter into a buttered and floured loaf pan, approximately 9-by-5-by-3 inches. Bake it in the center of the oven for 1 hour and 15 minutes.

7. Cool the loaf for 15 minutes in the pan; unmold the bread on a rack to cool it completely. Wrap it in plastic wrap and keep it a day before serving.

APPLESAUCE PECAN BREAD

Ruth Ellen Church

1 loaf

2 CUPS FLOUR
¾ CUP SUGAR
1 TABLESPOON BAKING POWDER
1 TEASPOON SALT
½ TEASPOON BAKING SODA
½ TEASPOON CINNAMON
1 CUP COARSELY CHOPPED
  PECANS OR WALNUTS
1 EGG, LIGHTLY BEATEN
1 CUP CANNED APPLESAUCE
2 TABLESPOONS MELTED BUTTER
  OR OIL

1. Preheat the oven to 350 F.

2. Measure the dry ingredients into a sifter. Sift them into a mixing bowl and stir in the nuts lightly. Combine the egg, applesauce and butter or oil. Add to the dry ingredients all at once and stir until it is just blended.

3. Spread it in a greased loaf pan, about 8-by-4-by-4 inches, and bake 50 minutes or slightly longer, until a cake tester or toothpick inserted in the center comes out clean. Cool it on a rack.

Note: For easy slicing, wrap the loaf in plastic wrap and refrigerate it for a day or so. It is delicious plain or with cream cheese.

ZUCCHINI BREAD WITH SUNFLOWER SEEDS

Paula J. Buchholz

2 loaves

3 EGGS
1 CUP SALAD OIL
1 CUP SUGAR
1 TEASPOON VANILLA
1 TEASPOON LEMON FLAVORING
2 CUPS SHREDDED FRESH
  ZUCCHINI
1 CAN (8¼ OUNCES) CRUSHED
  PINEAPPLE, DRAINED

3 CUPS ALL-PURPOSE FLOUR
2 TEASPOONS BAKING SODA
1½ TEASPOONS GROUND
  CINNAMON
¾ TEASPOON GROUND NUTMEG
¼ TEASPOON SALT
1 CUP RAISINS
1 CUP SHELLED SUNFLOWER
  SEEDS

1. Preheat the oven to 350 F.

2. Beat the eggs with the oil, sugar, vanilla and lemon flavoring until they are thick.

3. Stir in the zucchini, pineapple, flour, baking soda, cinnamon, nutmeg and salt, blending them well. Then fold in the raisins and sunflower seeds.

4. Pour the batter into two oiled and floured 9-by-5-inch loaf pans and bake in the preheated oven until a cake tester inserted in the center of the loaves comes out clean, about 1 hour.

5. Cool the loaves for 15 minutes before removing them from the pans; complete the cooling on a rack.

BUTTERMILK SCONES

Nan Mabon

6 to 8 scones

1 CUP FLOUR
½ TEASPOON BAKING SODA
½ TEASPOON CREAM OF TARTAR
½ TEASPOON BAKING POWDER
1 TABLESPOON SUGAR
2 TABLESPOONS BUTTER
  (PREFERABLY UNSALTED)
½ CUP BUTTERMILK
1 TEASPOON COOKING OIL

1. Sift the flour, baking soda, cream of tartar, baking powder and sugar into a mixing bowl.

2. Using your fingertips, rub 1 tablespoon of the butter into the dry ingredients, then stir in the buttermilk. The dough should be soft and moist at this point.

3. Turn the dough out onto a well-floured board, handling the dough as little as possible. Roll it out very lightly to a thickness of about ¾ inch. Then cut the dough into small circles with a cookie cutter or glass.

4. Melt the remaining 1 tablespoon of butter in a cast-iron skillet, along with the teaspoon of cooking oil. When the butter is hot, put in the scones and cook them about 3 minutes on each side. Wrap them in a clean cloth to keep them warm and soft. Serve with jam.

BANANA-NUT BREAD

Paul Rubinstein

1 loaf

9 TABLESPOONS (1 STICK PLUS 1
   TABLESPOON) SOFTENED BUTTER
2 CUPS PLUS 1 TABLESPOON
   ALL-PURPOSE FLOUR
1 CUP LIGHT BROWN SUGAR
   (FIRMLY PACKED TO MEASURE)
2 EGGS
½ TEASPOON SALT
½ TEASPOON DOUBLE-ACTING
   BAKING POWDER

2 CUPS JUST-RIPE BANANAS,
   LIQUEFIED IN A BLENDER OR
   THOROUGHLY MASHED (ABOUT 3
   MEDIUM-SIZED BANANAS)
⅔ CUP CHOPPED ALMONDS AND
   WALNUTS (PROPORTIONS
   OPTIONAL)

1. Preheat the oven to 350 F.

2. Using 1 tablespoon of butter, grease a 12-by-3-by-4½-inch loaf pan and then dust it with 1 tablespoon of flour, shaking out and discarding the excess flour. (You may use two loaf pans approximately half the size given.)

3. In the bowl of an electric mixer, cream together the remaining butter and the brown sugar at medium speed.

4. Break the eggs into a small bowl and beat them with a fork or whisk just enough to blend the yolks and whites without foaming.

5. When the butter-sugar mixture is smooth, add the beaten eggs to the mixing bowl and beat well at high speed.

6. Reduce the speed to medium, sift together the 2 cups of flour, salt and baking powder, and add to the mixture a little at a time. Continue mixing until it is well blended.

7. Beat in the liquefied bananas.

8. Turn off the mixer, and stir in the chopped nuts, distributing them as evenly as possible throughout.

9. Pour the mixture into the loaf pan and bake it for 1 hour, or until golden brown and puffed up.

10. Pass a sharp knife around the edges of the loaf pan and reserve onto a cooling rack. Allow the bread to cool before slicing and serving.

BACON MUFFINS

Jeanne Lesem

6 small muffins

2 SLICES BACON
3 CUPS SIFTED ALL-PURPOSE
  FLOUR
3 TABLESPOONS SIFTED WHOLE
  WHEAT FLOUR
1½ TEASPOONS BAKING POWDER
¼ TEASPOON SALT
1 TO 2 TABLESPOONS SUGAR
1 MEDIUM EGG
½ CUP MILK
2 TABLESPOONS BACON FAT,
  MELTED BUTTER OR VEGETABLE
  OIL

Try!

1. Preheat the oven to 400 F.

2. Line a 6-unit muffin pan with paper or foil cups or grease each indentation lightly with vegetable shortening.

3. Place the bacon in a small skillet, set it over low heat, and fry, turning occasionally, while mixing the batter. When it is crisp and brown, remove the bacon to drain on paper towels and reserve the fat.

4. Sift the all-purpose and whole wheat flours, the baking powder, salt and sugar together into a mixing bowl of at least 1½-pint capacity. Crumble the bacon into the dry ingredients, and toss lightly with a spoon or fork to keep it from clumping.

5. Beat the egg lightly, just to mix, and add it and the milk all at once to the dry ingredients. Add the melted bacon fat. Stir it with a fork only until all the flour is moistened. The mixture should be lumpy.

6. Divide the batter among the muffin cups, and bake on the middle shelf of the oven for 15 minutes, or until well risen and a muffin tests done (a small skewer or toothpick stuck in the center should emerge with no sticky batter clinging to it.)

7. Serve hot with butter and jam or jelly or preserves.

Breads: Savory, Filled and Otherwise

PESTO PIZZA

Florence Fabricant

2 10-inch pizzas

The recipe for pesto yields more than you will need to make the pesto pizza. The sauce keeps beautifully, either refrigerated or frozen. It makes a delicious sauce for pasta or serve it with fresh tomato slices.

Pesto (2 cups):
1½ CUPS CHOPPED FRESH BASIL
  LEAVES, PACKED
½ CUP PINE NUTS
2 LARGE CLOVES GARLIC
¾ CUP OLIVE OIL
⅓ CUP FRESHLY GRATED
  PARMESAN CHEESE
1 TEASPOON SALT
¼ TEASPOON FRESHLY GROUND
  PEPPER

1. Combine all the ingredients in a blender jar and blend until smooth.

1 PACKAGE ACTIVE DRY YEAST
1 CUP WARM WATER
PINCH OF SUGAR
2 TABLESPOONS OLIVE OIL
1 TEASPOON SALT
½ TEASPOON FRESHLY GROUND
  BLACK PEPPER (COARSELY
  GROUND IF POSSIBLE)

3 CUPS ALL-PURPOSE FLOUR
  (APPROXIMATELY)
CORNMEAL
¼ CUP PESTO
1 CUP SHREDDED MOZZARELLA
  CHEESE
½ CUP FRESHLY GRATED
  PARMESAN CHEESE

1. In a large bowl, dissolve the yeast in the water mixed with sugar and allow it to proof (the mixture should become frothy). Add the olive oil, salt and pepper to the yeast. Stir in the flour gradually, until the dough leaves the sides of the bowl.

2. Turn the dough out onto a floured board and knead it until it is smooth and very elastic (about 10 minutes), kneading in additional flour if necessary.

3. Place the dough in an oiled bowl, turning the dough to coat it with oil on all sides. Cover the dough and allow it to rise until doubled in bulk.

4. Punch down the dough and divide it into two equal portions.

5. Preheat the oven to 500 F.

6. Sprinkle the cornmeal on a baking sheet or a 10-inch pizza pan. Roll and stretch one of the portions of the dough into a circle about 10 inches in diameter, leaving a thicker rim around the edge. Place the dough on the baking sheet or in the pan and repeat the procedure with the second portion of dough.

7. Spread each circle with 2 tablespoons of the pesto, ½ cup of the mozzarella and ¼ cup of the Parmesan cheese.

8. Bake the pizzas for about 20 minutes, until the crust is brown. Cut the pizzas into wedges and serve. (For a very crisp crust, remove the pizzas from the pan and place them directly on the oven rack for a minute or two.)

ROMANO CHEESE STRAWS

Carole Lalli

3 dozen

2 CUPS FLOUR
½ TEASPOON SALT
¼ TEASPOON WHITE PEPPER
⅛ TEASPOON FRESHLY GRATED
  NUTMEG
3 DROPS TABASCO AND/OR PINCH
  OF CAYENNE PEPPER
8 TABLESPOONS (1 STICK) BUTTER

2⅔ TABLESPOONS LARD
⅓ CUP ICE WATER
1 LARGE EGG
1 TABLESPOON DIJON-STYLE
  MUSTARD
1½ CUPS FINELY GRATED ROMANO
  CHEESE

1. Combine the flour and the seasonings. Using your fingers or a pastry blender, quickly cut in the butter and lard. Stir in just enough of the water to hold the dough together. Do not overwork it. Divide the dough into two balls, sprinkle with flour, wrap them tightly in plastic wrap and refrigerate for several hours or overnight.

2. Preheat the oven to 400 F.

3. Roll the dough into sheets ¼-inch thick. Brush the dough with the egg beaten with the mustard. Sprinkle the grated cheese over the surface of the dough and press gently in place with your fingers or a spatula. Using a pastry cutter or knife, cut the dough into strips about ½-inch wide by 4 to 6 inches long. Twist each strip several times and place it on a buttered baking sheet.

4. Bake for 7 to 10 minutes, being careful not to allow the straws to burn. They should be just lightly browned. Recrisp, if necessary, in a 200 F. oven. Serve these with drinks or with soup.

CAUCASIAN CHEESE BREAD (KHACHAPURI)

Ruth Spear

1 very large loaf serving 14 to 18

Pirozhki **Yeast Dough:**
1 PACKAGE ACTIVE DRY YEAST
¼ CUP LUKEWARM WATER
1 TEASPOON PLUS 2
   TABLESPOONS SUGAR
3¼ CUPS SCALDED MILK
8 TABLESPOONS (1 STICK) BUTTER
1½ TEASPOONS SALT
4 CUPS FLOUR
2 EGGS PLUS 1 EGG YOLK

1. In a small bowl, proof the yeast in the water with 1 teaspoon of sugar for 10 minutes.

2. In a large bowl, combine the milk, butter, 2 tablespoons sugar and salt and beat until the butter is melted. Let the mixture cool to lukewarm. Gradually add 2 cups of the flour and beat the mixture until it is smooth.

3. Place the eggs and egg yolk in a small bowl; beat them lightly. Add the yeast mixture and eggs to the dough and beat for 2 minutes. Add the remaining 2 cups of flour and knead with a dough hook until the mass is smooth and satiny for about 5 minutes, or 10 minutes if you knead it by hand.

4. Remove the dough from the bowl and knead it briefly. Form it into a ball and place it in a buttered bowl. Film the top of the dough with melted butter. Cover the bowl with plastic wrap and chill it for at least 4 hours or overnight.

1 RECIPE *PIROZHKI* YEAST DOUGH
CORNMEAL
2 POUNDS *HAVARTI* OR *FONTAL*
   CHEESE
2 EGGS, LIGHTLY BEATEN
3 TABLESPOONS MELTED BUTTER,
   COOLED
2 TEASPOONS CRUSHED
   CORIANDER SEEDS
½ TEASPOON WHITE PEPPER
1 EGG BEATEN WITH 2
   TABLESPOONS HEAVY CREAM
   FOR A WASH

1. Punch down the chilled yeast dough and roll it out into a 20-inch circle on a lightly floured surface. Fold the circle lightly into quarters and place the center point of the folded circle in the center of a 9-inch pie plate, which has been buttered and sprinkled with cornmeal.

2. Unfold the dough, letting it drape over the edges and press it lightly into the plate.

3. Grate the cheese and combine it with the eggs, the melted butter, coriander and pepper. Spread the cheese filling over the dough, mounding it slightly in

the center. Gather the edges of the dough up as you would a cloth, pleating it in loose, even folds. When it is all together in your hand, twist it into a small knot.

4. Preheat the oven to 350 F.

5. Put the bread in a warm, draft-free spot, covered, to rise again for 20 minutes or so. Brush it with the egg wash and bake on the low shelf of the oven for 1 hour or until golden. Let the bread cool in the pan for 10 minutes, then transfer it to a bread board and serve hot, cut into wedges.

SAUSAGE BREAD (PANE CON SALSICCI)

Nicola Zanghi

1 loaf

⅔ PACKAGE ACTIVE DRY YEAST
½ TEASPOON SALT
1 CUP WARM WATER
2 CUPS SIFTED ALL-PURPOSE
   FLOUR
1 TABLESPOON FENNEL SEEDS
OLIVE OIL
1½ POUNDS FENNEL-FLAVORED
   ITALIAN SAUSAGES IN LINKS
EGG

1. Mix the yeast and salt in the water. Let it stand 5 minutes.

2. Add the flour and fennel seeds. Mix together and form the dough into a ball. Place the dough in a bowl, rub the olive oil on top, cover it with a cloth and let it rise. Punch down the dough and let it rise again.

3. Remove the dough from the bowl, flour a work surface and gently knead the dough to an elongated oval shape. Let it rest 15 to 20 minutes.

4. Cover the sausages with cold water and bring them to a boil. Prick the casing with a fork and allow the sausage to simmer, covered, for 10 minutes. Drain and pat them dry.

5. Preheat the oven to 400 F.

6. Place the sausage links in the center of the oval loaf and roll the dough around the sausage. Carefully knead the seam together.

7. Place the loaf on a baking pan and make three 3-inch-long, ¼-inch-deep diagonal slashes on top of the loaf with a sharp knife. Brush the top lightly with the egg beaten with 2 teaspoons of water. Bake the loaf until it is lightly browned (approximately 35 minutes).

8. Lower the oven temperature to 350 F. and bake for an additional 10 to 12 minutes, until it is brown.

SAVORY ITALIAN TURNOVERS (PETONI)

Nicola Zanghi

12 to 15 turnovers

Ingredients for Dough:
1 PACKAGE DRY ACTIVE YEAST
1 CUP LUKEWARM WATER
1 TEASPOON SALT
1 TABLESPOON BUTTER
(PREFERABLY UNSALTED)
3 CUPS SIFTED ALL-PURPOSE
FLOUR
1 EGG

Ingredients for Filling and Final Preparation:
½ POUND BACON, DICED
½ CUP DICED SCALLIONS, WHITE
PART ONLY
¼ CUP OLIVE OIL
1 POUND FRESH LEAF SPINACH
1 POUND CAN PEELED PLUM
TOMATOES, COARSELY CHOPPED
2 HARD-COOKED EGGS, CHOPPED
½ CUP CHOPPED BLACK OLIVES
6 ANCHOVY FILLETS, CHOPPED
¼ CUP GRATED PARMESAN
CHEESE
½ POUND MOZZARELLA CHEESE
CUT INTO ¼-INCH CUBES
VEGETABLE OIL

To Prepare Dough:
1. In a large mixing bowl, dissolve the yeast in warm water. Let it stand for 5 minutes and stir.

2. Add the salt and butter to the yeast, mixing thoroughly, then blend in 1½ cups of flour.

3. Add the remaining flour and the egg, mixing only enough to blend. Knead the dough until smooth, form it into a ball and place it in a bowl and rub olive oil on top of the dough so that a skin does not form. Let it stand, covered with a dry cloth, in a warm area for ½ hour.

Meanwhile Prepare Filling:
1. In a large skillet, sauté the bacon until it is lightly crisp. Reserve it. Discard the fat and wipe out the skillet.

2. Over medium heat, sauté the scallions in ¼ cup of olive oil until they are translucent. Add the bacon, spinach and tomatoes and cook until the spinach wilts.

3. Transfer the mixture to a large mixing bowl and stir in the hard-cooked eggs, olives, anchovies and the cheeses until they are uniformly blended.

To Assemble:
1. Generously flour a work surface and roll the dough to a thickness of ¼ inch. Let it rest for 10 minutes.

2. With a sharp knife, cut the dough into 5-by-5-inch squares.

3. In the center of each square, place a small ball (approximately 2 tablespoons) of the filling. Fold each square along the diagonal; crimp down the edges with fork tines.

4. Heat equal parts of vegetable and olive oil over medium heat, using enough to form a ½-inch layer of oil in the skillet. Dust the excess flour off the *petoni*. Fry them until lightly browned on both sides, turning over twice.

BRIOCHE WITH HAM AND CHEESE
(BRIOCHE MOUSSELINE LIVERNOIS)

Raymond Sokolov

1 large and 1 small brioche

5 TO 5½ CUPS SIFTED FLOUR
2 PACKAGES ACTIVE DRY YEAST
⅔ CUP LUKEWARM MILK
  (APPROXIMATELY)
7 EGGS
1 TABLESPOON SALT
1 PINCH SUGAR
14 OUNCES (3½ STICKS) SOFTENED
  BUTTER (PREFERABLY UNSALTED)
¼ POUND SWISS CHEESE, DICED
¼ POUND HAM, DICED

1. Make a circle on your work surface with roughly one-quarter of the flour. Put the yeast in the center of the circle. Pour a small amount of the milk on the yeast and stir together until the yeast is dissolved. Add more milk and mix in the circle of flour so as to make a homogeneous, smooth ball of dough. Set this ball to rise in a covered bowl in a warm, moist place until it doubles in volume.

2. When the first rise is complete, make a second circle of flour with the remaining flour. Put 4 eggs and 2 tablespoons of milk in the middle. Mix together into a ball and work briefly.

3. Dissolve the salt and sugar in a small amount of milk or warm water and work into the dough from the previous step. Also work in the butter and 2 of the remaining eggs. Then knead in the cheese, the ham and, finally, the ball of risen yeast dough. During this whole process, you should be kneading and breaking the dough quite actively. Continue kneading until the dough is elastic and begins to blister. Set it aside to rise. When the dough has doubled in bulk, refrigerate it until ready to bake.

4. Butter the inside of an 8-cup cylindrical mold (or a 2-pound coffee can), as well as one regular, large brioche mold (about 5 cups).

5. Punch down the dough and divide it so as to fill both molds two-thirds full. Let the dough rise until the molds are full.

6. Preheat the oven to 350 F.

7. Tie a paper collar around the cylindrical mold so that the top of the paper rises 3 inches above the top of the mold. Beat the remaining egg and brush the top of each brioche. Bake the small mold for 25 minutes, and the large mold for 40 minutes.

8. Cool each loaf on a rack for 5 minutes before unmolding. Serve as an accompaniment to an omelet, salad, soup or other light lunch.

NO-KNEAD DILL BREAD

Carol Cutler

1 round loaf

Even though this is not a sweet bread, I like to serve it as a coffee cake for the afternoon break. It also graces the breakfast table, usually toasted. At dinner time, pair it with fish soup to discover an inspired combination. The perky smell of the dill sets taste buds tingling; a palate promise that is more than fulfilled. With just a few minor alterations this no-knead bread can become a low-cholesterol favorite. A lot of mileage for a bread that is done in a flash.

1 PACKAGE ACTIVE DRY YEAST
(¼ OUNCE) OR 1 CAKE (.6
OUNCE) COMPRESSED YEAST
¼ CUP WARM WATER
1 CUP SMALL CURD COTTAGE
CHEESE
3 TABLESPOONS BUTTER
2 TABLESPOONS HONEY
1 TEASPOON DRIED ONION SOUP
2 TEASPOONS DILL WEED
¼ TEASPOON BAKING SODA
1 TEASPOON SALT
1 BEATEN EGG
2¼ TO 2½ CUPS FLOUR

1. In a large mixing bowl, soften the yeast in the warm water; stir to dissolve the yeast.

2. In a saucepan, heat the cottage cheese, 1 tablespoon of butter, and the honey until they are lukewarm. Add to the cottage cheese mixture the dried onion soup, dill weed, baking soda, salt and the egg. Stir to blend all the flavorings.

3. Scrape the cottage cheese mixture into the yeast and water and stir it again. Add enough flour to make a firm ball of dough; stir it with a wooden spoon but do not knead. Soak a cloth with hot water, wring it out, and place it over the mixing bowl. Let the dough rise in a warm place until it has doubled in bulk, about 1 hour.

4. Stir down the dough. Use 1 tablespoon of butter to grease an 8-inch-round cake pan and put the dough in the pan, patting to smooth it a little. Let it rise for about 45 minutes.

5. Preheat the oven to 350 F.

6. Place the baking pan in the oven and bake for 40 to 50 minutes, or until the top is nicely browned. Cool the bread slightly, then remove it to a rack. To achieve a shiny crust, melt the remaining tablespoon of butter and brush it over the top.

Notes: 1) No-knead dill bread freezes perfectly. It is best to cut it into thick slices before freezing. 2) For the low-cholesterol variation, use low-fat cottage cheese, substituting 4 tablespoons of polyunsaturated margarine for the 3 tablespoons of butter, and add the extra margarine to the batter; use 2 egg whites instead of the beaten egg.

INDIAN FLAT BREAD WITH SPINACH
(PARATHAS)

Raymond Sokolov

10 to 12 *parathas*

4 CUPS SIFTED WHOLE WHEAT
  FLOUR
2 CUPS WATER (APPROXIMATELY)
1 10-OUNCE PACKAGE FRESH
  SPINACH
2 MEDIUM-SIZED ONIONS, PEELED
  AND CHOPPED
1 TABLESPOON CHILI POWDER
1 TABLESPOON GROUND CUMIN
1½ TABLESPOONS SALT
½ POUND (2 STICKS) BUTTER
  (PREFERABLY UNSALTED)

1. Mix the flour with 1 cup of water in a bowl. If necessary, add more water, ¼ cup at a time, until the dough forms a smooth mass that does not stick to the sides of the bowl. This is a dry dough. Stop adding water as soon as it becomes workable.

2. Turn the dough out onto a lightly floured surface and knead it for 15 minutes.

3. Wash and dry the spinach and chop it. Knead the spinach, onions, chili powder, cumin and salt into the dough. Cover the dough with a damp towel and allow it to rest for 1 to 2 hours.

4. Meanwhile, melt the butter over medium heat. When it boils, turn the heat as low as possible and continue cooking it until all the white milk solids have dropped to the bottom and left the surface of the butter clear. This will take about 30 minutes. Then, pour off the clarified butter, or *ghee,* through a fine strainer lined with cheesecloth into a heatproof container. Reserve it and do not refrigerate if you will be using it the same day.

5. When the dough has rested, divide it into 10 or 12 balls the size of medium-small lemons. Roll out each of them into 5-inch circles. Brush the surface of each circle with the *ghee.* Fold in half, into semicircles and brush the tops with more *ghee.* Fold them over again, into quarter-circles.

6. Brush a heavy griddle or skillet with the *ghee.* Heat over moderate heat until water sprinkled onto the *ghee* will pop.

7. Roll out 1 quarter-circle until it has doubled in area, keeping the triangular shape. Put the triangle on the griddle.

8. While the *paratha* fries, brush the top with *ghee.* When brown spots appear on the bottom (check by picking up a corner with a spatula), turn, brush the other side with *ghee* and turn again when brown spots appear underneath. After 5 seconds, remove the *paratha* from the pan and drain it on paper toweling. Continue in this manner until you have fried all the *parathas.*

BREAD BASKET (CROUSTADE)

Julie Dannenbaum

1 "basket"

1 LOAF UNSLICED, HOMESTYLE
   BREAD
8 TABLESPOONS (1 STICK) MELTED
   BUTTER

1. Preheat the oven to 325 F.

2. With a serrated knife, slice off the top of the loaf of bread, horizontally, cutting down 1½ inches.

3. Remove the insides of the bread by cutting in 1 inch all the way around the loaf, leaving a shell.

4. Using a pastry brush, brush the shell with the butter, inside and out, and place it on a baking sheet.

5. Place the shell in the oven, on the middle shelf, and bake slowly for 30 to 45 minutes, or until the bread is firm and golden. Use the shell as a basket to serve scrambled eggs with chives and mushrooms, creamed dried beef or chicken, or fried oysters.

Note: The top and the scooped out insides of the bread can be ground in the blender or food processor for crumbs.

HERBED MELBA

Julie Dannenbaum

This is a practical method for using up day-old rolls or bread.

DAY OLD ROLLS OR BREAD
MELTED BUTTER
MIXED HERBS TO TASTE (A
   COMBINATION OF PARSLEY,
   THYME AND CHIVES)

1. Preheat the oven to 325 F.

2. Slice the bread or rolls ¼-inch thick.

3. Brush each slice with melted butter, on both sides, using a pastry brush.

4. Lay the slices side by side on a baking sheet.

5. Sprinkle herbs to taste over each piece.

6. Bake them in the oven for 30 to 45 minutes, turning the slices half way through. Serve these toasts with soup. They will freeze.

EDITORS

Arnold Goldman
Barbara Spiegel
Lyn Stallworth

EDITORIAL ASSISTANTS

Christopher Carter
Susan Lipke

EDITORIAL CONSULTANTS

Wendy Afton Rieder
Kate Slate

CONTRIBUTORS

Introduction by Irene Sax

Michael Batterberry, author of several books on food, art and social history, is also a painter, and is editor and food critic for a number of national magazines. He has taught at James Beard's cooking classes in New York and many of his original recipes have appeared in *House & Garden, House Beautiful* and *Harper's Bazaar.*

Paula J. Buchholz is the regional co-ordinator for the National Culinary Apprenticeship Program. She has been a food writer for the *Detroit Free Press* and for the *San Francisco Examiner.*

Giuliano Bugialli, author of *The Fine Art of Italian Cooking,* is co-founder and teacher of Cooking in Florence, a program conducted in Italy. He also has a cooking school in New York.

Vilma Liacouras Chantiles, author of *The Food of Greece,* writes a food and consumer column for the *Scarsdale* (New York) *Inquirer* and a monthly food column for *Athenian Magazine* (Athens, Greece).

Ruth Ellen Church, a syndicated wine columnist for the *Chicago Tribune,* had been food editor for that newspaper for more than thirty years when she recently retired. The author of seven cookbooks, her most recent book is *Entertaining with Wine.* Mrs. Church's *Wines and Cheese of the Midwest* will be published in the fall of 1977.

Elizabeth Colchie is a noted food consultant who has done extensive recipe development and testing as well as research into the history of foods and cookery. She was on the editorial staff of *The Cooks' Catalogue* and has written numerous articles for such magazines as *Gourmet, House & Garden* and *Family Circle.*

Carol Cutler, who has been a food columnist for the *Washington Post,* is a graduate of the Cordon Bleu and L'Ecole des Trois Gourmands in Paris. She is the author of *Haute Cuisine for Your Heart's Delight* and *The Six-Minute Soufflé and Other Culinary Delights.* She has also written for *House & Garden, American Home* and *Harper's Bazaar.*

Julie Dannenbaum is the founding Director of the largest non-professional cooking school in the country, the Creative Cooking School in Philadelphia. She is the author of *Julie Dannenbaum's Creative Cooking School* and *Menus for All Occasions.* She is also Director of the Gritti Palace Hotel Cooking School in Venice and The Grand Hotel Cooking School in Rome.

Nathalie Dupree has been Director of Rich's Cooking School in Atlanta, Georgia, since it opened in September, 1975. She has an Advanced Certificate from the London Cordon Bleu and has owned restaurants in Spain and Georgia.

Florence Fabricant is a free-lance writer, reporting on restaurants and food for *The New York Times, New York* magazine and other publications. She was on the staff of *The Cooks' Catalogue* and editor of the paperback edition.

Emanuel and Madeline Greenberg co-authored *Whiskey in the Kitchen* and are consultants to the food and beverage industry. Emanuel, a home economist, is a regular contributor to the food columns of *Playboy* magazine.

Diana Kennedy, the leading authority on the food of Mexico, is the author of *The Cuisines of Mexico* and *The Tortilla Book.*

Carole Lalli is a contributing editor to *New West* magazine and its restaurant reviewer. She formerly ran a catering business in New York.

Jeanne Lesem, Family Editor of United Press International, is the author of *The Pleasures of Preserving and Pickling.*

Nan Mabon, a free-lance food writer and cooking teacher in New York City, is also the cook for a private executive dining room on Wall Street. She studied at the Cordon Bleu in London.

Helen McCully is food editor of *House Beautiful* magazine and the author of many books on food, among them *Nobody Ever Tells You These Things About Food and Drink, Cooking with Helen McCully Beside You* and, most recently, *Waste Not, Want Not: A Cookbook of Delicious Foods from Leftovers.* She was a consultant on the staff of *The Cooks' Catalogue.*

Gloria Bley Miller is the author of *Learn Chinese Cooking in Your Own Kitchen* and *The Thousand Recipe Chinese Cookbook.*

Maurice Moore-Betty, owner-operator of The Civilized Art Cooking School, food consultant and restaurateur, is author of *Cooking for Occasions, The Maurice Moore-Betty Cooking School Book of Fine Cooking* and *The Civilized Art of Salad Making.*

Jane Moulton, a food writer for the *Plain Dealer* in Cleveland, took her degree in foods and nutrition. As well as reporting on culinary matters and reviewing food-related books for the *Plain Dealer,* she has worked in recipe development, public relations and catering.

Paul Rubinstein is the author of *Feasts for Two, The Night Before Cookbook* and *Feasts for Twelve* (*or More*). He is a stockbroker and the son of pianist Artur Rubinstein.

Raymond Sokolov, author of *The Saucier's Apprentice,* is a free-lance writer with a particular interest in food.

Ruth Spear is the author of *The East Hampton Cookbook* and writes occasional pieces on food for *New York* magazine. She is currently at work on a new cookbook.

Harvey Steiman is food editor of the *Miami Herald.* He has taught cooking classes and lectured on wine and restaurants at the Food and Hotel School of Florida International University.

Joanne Will is food editor of the *Chicago Tribune* and a member of three Chicago wine and food societies.

Nicola Zanghi is the owner-chef of Restaurant Zanghi in Glen Cove, New York. He started his apprenticeship under his father at the age of thirteen, and is a graduate of two culinary colleges. He is an instructor at the Cordon Bleu school in New York City.